Praise for
Good God, Lousy World, and Me

"Holly Burkhalter has been a voice of conscience in Washington for many, many years. She has written some of the most powerful and pointed op-eds the *Post* has published. She's a gifted writer with a big heart and a unique, compassionate take on the human condition."

—FRED HIATT of *The Washington Post*

"Holly's story, from a distance, is absolutely fascinating—one of the world's top experts in human rights turns out to be a person of deep Christian commitments. But her story up close is even better: by turns laugh-out-loud funny, poignant, wrenching, and hopeful. I think this is a voice the wider world needs to hear."

—ANDY CROUCH, author of *Culture Making: Recovering Our Creative Calling* and executive editor of *Christianity Today*

"*Good God, Lousy World, and Me* is what happens when a passion for justice is joined to a seeking spirit. Holly Burkhalter's work for a world that cherishes all people is undergirded by her faith in a God who does likewise. This is Christianity as we wish it could be."

—PHILLIP GULLEY, author of *Living the Quaker Way*

"*Good God, Lousy World, and Me* is a desperately needed, encouraging read, helping us see that we don't need everything figured out before we act on behalf of the poor, marginalized, and oppressed. Instead Holly takes us on a journey where true strength shows up through our humanity, where our daily burdens and spiritual questioning make faith the miracle it truly is. With a blunt, challenging, funny, and intimate recount of personal experiences, Holly punches some of the taboos left in today's society. For those of us who've questioned God after witnessing, hearing, or experiencing injustice or those who've quietly suffered with mental illness, Holly's words rally the soul and challenge the myth that one must accept neat answers to life's darkest moments before professing faith and declaring war on injustice."

—STEVE MARTIN, CEO of Love146

"Anything written by Holly Burkhalter is worth reading, and her book is no exception."

—JODY WILLIAMS, winner of the 1997 Nobel
Peace Prize

"Holly's story is a journey from unbelief to the unbelievably critical work of justice for the poor and marginalized in the name of God. It's a powerful story from an unforgettable pilgrim.

—JOEL EDWARDS, director of Micah Challenge
International

"In this extraordinary memoir of grace, one of the foremost human rights advocates of the last half century shares her brutally and hilariously honest story of finding God on one of the most unlikely, irreverent, and utterly beautiful pilgrimages through life as it actually is. Hers will become an iconic story of spiritual reflection in our era—a chronicle of the deepest human yearning amidst shattering pain, everyday redemption, and the irrepressible love of her Maker."

—GARY A. HAUGEN, president & CEO
of International Justice Mission

"Face to face with atrocities that call into question both the existence of God and 'is there any human left in humanity,' Holly comes out swinging. Intermittently humble and fierce, she dares to plumb the depths of faith and slowly, tenderly finds God. Living between winsome and raw, which is not for the faint of heart, there are tungsten strands of emerging faith. This book will leave you exhausted and exhilarated, both of which are good for expanding the soul."

NANCY ORTBERG, author of *Looking for God*

GOOD GOD

LOUSY WORLD

& ME

GOOD GOD LOUSY WORLD & ME

*The Improbable Journey
of a Human Rights Activist
from Unbelief to Faith*

HOLLY BURKHALTER

CONVERGENT
BOOKS

GOOD GOD, LOUSY WORLD, AND ME
PUBLISHED BY CONVERGENT

All Scripture quotations, unless otherwise indicated, are taken from the New Revised Standard Version of the Bible, copyright © 1989 by the Division of Christian Education of the National Council of the Churches of Christ in the USA. Used by permission. All rights reserved. Scripture quotations marked (KJV) are taken from the King James Version.

Details in some anecdotes and stories have been changed to protect the identities of the persons involved.

Hardcover ISBN 978-1-60142-508-9
eBook ISBN 978-1-60142-509-6

Copyright © 2013 by Holly Burkhalter

Cover design by Kristopher K. Orr
Cover photography by Frans Devriese

Published in the United States by Convergent, an imprint of the Crown Publishing Group, a division of Random House LLC, New York, a Penguin Random House Company.

CONVERGENT BOOKS and its open book colophon are trademarks of Random House LLC.

The Cataloging-in-Publication Data is on file with the Library of Congress.

Printed in the United States of America
2013—First Edition

10 9 8 7 6 5 4 3 2 1

SPECIAL SALES
Most Convergent books are available at special quantity discounts when purchased in bulk by corporations, organizations, and special-interest groups. Custom imprinting or excerpting can also be done to fit special needs. For information, please e-mail SpecialMarkets@ConvergentBooks.com or call 1-800-603-7051.

To Sharon

Contents

GOOD GOD

LOUSY WORLD

& ME

one

Tires on a Jeep

It was the year 1990. I was in West Africa and not happy about it. Thousands of Liberians had been forcibly displaced from their country by marauding army and rebel forces. Fleeing families were living in squalor, drinking and washing in filthy water, and eating whatever scraps poor villagers could share.

My assignment was to interview these refugees from hell and report on the events that had put them to flight.

In a quiet voice, a man described to me a fellow villager being slowly cut to death by teenage boys wearing women's wigs. A young woman explained that she'd survived an attack on her village by hiding in the bush, from where she watched armed men wrap her mother in a gasoline-soaked mattress and set it aflame. A university professor who had fled with only the clothes he wore—a business suit—wept while we spoke, bizarrely, of the indignity of eating with his hands. Having lost everything, he yearned for a fork.

I took notes, filling pages of my notebook with hideous, degrading, pitiful stories, one after another. Then I rejoined my fellow travelers, a group of American and French relief experts, for a jouncing Jeep ride through the bush back to our hostel in town.

When we arrived, one of my colleagues, an Ethiopian evangelical woman, broke into joyful prayer. She thanked the Lord for our safe arrival and for sparing our overland vehicle a flat tire.

I thought I'd vomit. I had literally overdosed on malaria medicine—a French doctor in the refugee camp told me, mistakenly, to double my dosage, so I did. Antimalarial drugs in those days caused hallucinations, and I was having them. I hadn't eaten or slept for three days, and I was trembling with revulsion and fear from the stories I'd heard. Praising God for our spectacular privileges, right down to our intact tires, in the face of the hunger and trauma we'd just witnessed, struck me as downright obscene. I wasn't a Christian at the beginning of that trip, and by the end of it I could scarcely tolerate the sight of those who were.

I'm not sure I was an atheist. No self-respecting atheist would bother to curse God daily for misery and injustice as vigorously as I did for forty years. I must have believed in *something* good to have felt so betrayed and heartbroken by every day's fresh load of cruelty and suffering around the world. I would think bitterly, "Thanks, God. Thanks a whole lot for *that*." And I don't think *agnostic* is the right word either, if that means I weighed the evidence for and against and couldn't form an opinion. I wanted there to be a God who was good and whose creation mirrored it, and it just wasn't there. So perhaps the term for me was "twisted, pissed-off, betrayed, former Christian." I can't find that in the dictionary, but it's what I was.

I once heard it said that you can believe in an all-powerful and loving God or you can believe in the Holocaust, but you cannot believe in both of those things. Yes. When I think of the Holocaust and other atrocities that have become horrifyingly ordinary, it seems just stupid to imagine a good God who put this in motion and only watches it unfold. He-she-or-it appears to be either uninterested or helpless against the forces of violence and cruelty that clearly have the upper hand most of the time, especially if you're a woman, a child, disabled, or poor. It's less painful to believe that the Creator doesn't exist at all than to witness the daily betrayal of everything a loving, sovereign God represents.

I didn't start out this way. I was born in 1954 to a devoutly Christian family. My grandparents were Mennonite missionaries in India, and we Burkhalters were committed churchgoers throughout my childhood. As a matter of fact, we sat through two services—sermon and all—every Sunday because my dad conducted the church choir. My parents were so respectful of their teetotaling religious roots that there wasn't a drop of alcohol in our house until I was in my late teens.

All of which is to say that we were steeped in Mennonite values, and church was the warp and woof of my childhood. I didn't have a very sophisticated grasp of Christianity, but it never occurred to me that God might be a colossal fake.

It became brutally clear that the whole business was fraudulent when my lovely grandfather died. He was an old man who had lived a good life in India as a pastor and then in gentle retirement in a sleepy Ohio town. But his death so devastated my grandmother that she had a mental breakdown. She, the most faithful of believers and devoted servants, lost her connection to the God she'd worshiped her whole life. She wept, asking out loud, "Where are you? Why did you leave me?" She lapsed into catatonic depression for a long time.

I was sixteen and I loved her very much. God's apparent

absence during her greatest need made me furious. What good, after all, was God if the minute somebody lost a loved one, he went AWOL? The choices were that God was indifferent to my grandmother's loss and sorrow, and thus a bad God, or he was aware of her suffering but powerless to help, and thus a weak God. The third choice was that he didn't exist and never had.

My grandmother's faith returned when she regained her mental health, but my faith, such as it was, certainly didn't. I basically ignored God until I started working in the international human rights field in the early 1980s. For the next thirty years, I was nose to nose with the worst things that human beings can do to one another. I worked first as a human rights staffer for Congress and then for Human Rights Watch and finally for Physicians for Human Rights. I loved those organizations and my work, but I got a sickening education in human beings' insatiable zest for raping, enslaving, torturing, and murdering those weaker than themselves.

It didn't help matters that many conservative churches in the United States harnessed themselves to a right-wing political agenda that I loathed. Jerry Falwell's Moral Majority was founded in 1979, the year I came to Washington to work for Congress. The politics of abortion, school prayer, creationism, and homosexuality roiled Capitol Hill. For liberals like me, the word *Christian* came to be synonymous with bigotry, exclusivity, and antiscientific fundamentalism.

But it was the Rwandan genocide of 1994 that cemented my horror of atrocities against the vulnerable and my cynicism about a good God. You remember. The country had just reached a peace agreement between Hutu and minority Tutsi Rwandans when the Rwandan president's plane was shot out of the sky by political extremists. To divert attention from their attempted putsch, Rwanda's politicians unleashed the army and the militias on unarmed citizens. They proceeded to terrify ordinary Hutu Rwandans into systematically and thoroughly exterminating almost every Tutsi in the country.

My colleagues at Human Rights Watch tried so hard to make a difference. The organization meticulously monitored and reported the carnage as village after village was engulfed in butchery. We published dozens of editorials in prominent newspapers, lobbied Congress, and met with top officials in the US government and the UN Security Council. We begged for the civilized countries of the world to intervene. It wouldn't have taken much. A couple thousand well-armed soldiers in armored vehicles moving across a country the size of Maryland would have ended the killing promptly. That's what we asked for, in hundreds of press releases, interviews, meetings, and letters.

None of our efforts staunched the slaughter, however. UN peacekeeping forces were drawn down to a tiny observer mission that had neither the weapons, the vehicles, nor the mandate to stop the killings. One hundred days later, eight hundred thousand children, women, and men had been butchered. Rwanda was a reeking abattoir and the clearest evidence of human depravity and God's indifference I'd seen in my lifetime. The genocide, like the Holocaust before it, blew up the way we thought about the world and God's place in it. For me, it was the ultimate evidence that God was either dead, weak, or couldn't have cared less. No sovereign, loving God would have watched passively while fathers, mothers, babies, toddlers, and grandparents were dispatched with clubs and machetes.

I was sick with fury. To me, believing in God was not only foolish, but it would have felt like I was breaking faith with all those Rwandan children, women, and men he had abandoned. You can see their skeletons to this day, piled up in the churches where they sought refuge and were subsequently beaten, raped, and slashed as they cowered in the pews.

The genocide was also the lowest point in my career in international human rights. I never imagined I had superpowers, but I did take seriously my specific job, which was to persuade US policymakers to do something—anything—to stop the killings in Rwanda. I believed with every fiber of my being that words would help. I believed that once people in power knew what was happening, they would stop the slaughter. I thought that telling the truth and sounding the alarm would change things. I was at the top of my game as a human rights advocate. But you know what? In terms of effectiveness, I might as well have been a gnat. A fruit fly. A dust mote. I never again felt the same about human rights advocacy.

While I was emotionally disengaging from my work, my heart became deeply entangled elsewhere. At the age of forty it occurred to me that something was badly missing from my husband John's and my life. I really was that middle-aged woman in the cartoon who screams, "I forgot to have children!" Actually, I had always loved children; I just never wanted any of my own. My own doubts and insecurities, not to mention a bad case of anxiety, had ruled out motherhood for me. About a decade of work with a superb psychologist brought me to a place where I not only knew that John and I would be great parents but we longed to be. We set out to produce a family.

Ah yes, and how un-fun it was. Fertility treatment was expensive, embarrassing, and painful. Fortunately for John and me, it was completely ineffective as well. We changed course, and in November 1995 we adopted four-month-old Grace Bofa from Anhui Province, China. When an orphanage official put her in my arms, my first thought was, *You are the most beautiful creature I have ever seen, and you definitely have the biggest ears.* My second thought was, *I do not know what I ever did to deserve this miracle. But I am so very grateful. Whoever you are, thank you for giving us this baby girl.*

It wasn't a prayer exactly, but it was the beginning of a dif-

ferent way of thinking about the world and about God. Whoever created Gracie, saved her life when she was found at one
week of age, and brought her to us in the middle of China
as a tiny, breathtakingly lovely baby had to be very, very good.
I didn't know whom to thank, but I was overwhelmingly
grateful.

Two years later we adopted Josie Bao-Ngan from Viet-
nam. I couldn't imagine loving another child as much as I
loved Grace, but it turned out I was an idiot. Josie, whom I
met at Dulles Airport when she arrived with an adoption
agency official, had apparently screamed throughout the entire
flight. She was five months old and sick, skinny, and scared.
She stared soberly into my face with her enormous black eyes,
then clung to me without letting go for the next twenty-four
hours, like a baby gibbon. We fell in love on the spot.

My husband and I had the girls baptized Catholic at
nearby St. Peter's Church. Not an obvious choice for me, a
leftist, feminist, faux atheist, but John is a cradle Catholic, and
he wanted to sign up his daughters. Since I didn't have any
faith of my own, it seemed like the thing to do. I rationalized
that when the kids became teenagers and it came time to reject
someone, they would pick the pope instead of me. I didn't realize that the fine print of baptizing children Catholic is that
one is expected to *raise* them Catholic. St. Peter's lovely old
pastor, Michael O'Sullivan, recognizing that fellow Irishman
John Fitzpatrick was the Catholic in our household, grabbed

him by the scruff of the neck after the baptism and said, "I'd better see you in church."

And thus we joined and have been going there for the past seventeen years. I made my peace with a church whose positions on certain social issues I despised by cleverly joining the choir. Instead of sitting in the pews, feeling like a stranger in a strange land, I got to be up in the loft with twenty other singers. If the homily got under my liberal skin, I could slip down to the basement and have coffee with the homeless guys until it was time to sing the anthem.

I went to St. Peter's every Sunday for about nine years before I became a Christian. I experienced many good things there: community, friendship, music, liturgy, beauty. But I did not encounter God. Looking over the balcony rail above the congregation, I would watch a sea of people who were intently listening to some voice I couldn't hear. If you aren't a believer, the language of faith is as unintelligible as Serbo-Croatian.

I knew why I was there: because my husband and kids are Catholic and I'm an alto. If I'd bailed, I'd have disappointed our choir director and my buddies in the alto section. But why were all the others there? I was completely bewildered at the sight of my Capitol Hill neighbors who gave up their Sunday mornings to worship a God I didn't believe in, experiencing something foreign to me. I saw that my beloved choirmates had joy and contentment that I didn't have, and I couldn't figure it out. It made me bitter, all those years ago, that God's presence was so readily available to everybody but me. And sometimes it still does.

But after those nine years of churchgoing atheism, my views about God in the world gradually started to change. Probably the biggest factor was my friendship with Gary Haugen, who visited my office at Human Rights Watch in 1996 to talk about starting up a new human rights group: International Justice Mission. Gary was an earnest Christian, and boy howdy did he look it in his dark suit with his absurd 1950s buzz-cut hair. But for some reason, I liked and trusted him.

The Rwanda genocide was our immediate point of connection. Paradoxically, the same Rwanda genocide that had me cursing an absent God had led Gary Haugen to create IJM. He was a civil rights lawyer with the Justice Department in 1994, and he was loaned to the United Nations just after the killings ended to do the first international investigation of the genocide. It was amid the reeking corpses of Kigali (the Rwandan capital) that Gary, as a believer in a good God, formed the intention to do something to bring protection and justice to the poorest and most vulnerable people in Rwanda.

His vision of a Christian organization that could animate previously silent American churches to speak out against violence was compelling. We didn't have it in the human rights movement, but it was desperately needed. And I loved his plan to recruit lawyers and investigators to provide services directly to victims of rape, child prostitution, and illegal imprisonment.

After talking and writing about human rights violations for two decades, I was entranced by the idea that somebody might actually do something to help even a few victims.

Gary launched IJM from the basement of his little town house in Arlington. He and his hilarious wife, Jan, had four kids under the age of four, and John and our girls and I became friends with their whole family. I watched the organization grow while I worked at another human rights group, and I helped on the fringes when I could.

Gary and I met often. Knowing he was a Christian, I bombarded him with questions about why the God he believed in was so noticeably absent from the lousy world around us. One day we were having coffee at my office and talking, as always, about the Rwanda genocide. As much as I liked Gary, I was incensed that he believed in a God who had allowed it. He thought for a long time and then said, "I don't know why God allowed the genocide in Rwanda. But I know that death is not all he has in store for all those children who were murdered. He will wipe away every tear from their eyes." I didn't believe it, but it lodged somewhere in the back of my brain, all the same.

Years later I heard Gary preach at a church on Capitol Hill. It was the kind of happy-clappy evangelical church I wouldn't have been caught dead in a few years before, but IJM friends invited me to hear his sermon. And there, for the first time, I actually got it about the spiritual underpinnings of the little organization that had come to mean so much to me. I had known all along that Gary founded IJM because he wanted, as a Christian, to serve God by securing protection for the poor from violence. But we had never talked about what Gary called in his sermon the "unfamiliar passions of God." He was referring to God's hatred of injustice, violence, and exploitation of the poor. As he put it, God has a plan to fight injustice, and that plan is us—his people. There is no Plan B.

Gary's authority for this is no less than the Bible:

Seek justice, rescue the oppressed, defend the orphan, plead for the widow.

Remember those who are in prison, as though you were in prison with them; those who are being tortured, as though you yourselves were being tortured.

Speak out for those who cannot speak, for the rights of all the destitute. Speak out, judge righteously, defend the rights of the poor and needy.

I never knew these passages even existed, much less that living, breathing Christians took them literally. I didn't believe in God or the Bible when I heard Gary's sermon, but "speaking up, judging fairly, and defending the rights of the poor and needy" were the things I had devoted my life to as an international human rights activist. To hear Gary challenge Christians to join a movement to end violence against the poor, using Scripture to justify it—indeed, command it—made me want to leap up and start waving my arms like a Pentecostal at a tent revival.

That radical, courageous, outrageous notion that God sees cruelty and demands that those who love him do something about it was the beginning of the end for my intellectual defenses against the concept of a kind God in a hurting world. IJM taught me that the atrocities that broke my heart broke God's more. I had for my entire life been cursing an absent God for suffering, but now I had to rethink it: maybe God wasn't absent after all. And because the Bible spoke so accurately about abuses against the weak and vulnerable—something I knew to be true in the present day—I had to think differently about the Bible as well, or at least bits of it. Seeing this sturdy group of Christians take completely seriously God's commandment to protect the poor turned my head around about Christians per se. These excellent people did not worship a bad God, an absent God, or a weak one. They worshiped a good God and wanted to do his bidding in a cruel and unjust world.

I wouldn't say I was a quick study. I had known Gary and his IJM colleagues for a decade before I came to believe in their God just seven or eight years ago. But their faith and work to protect the vulnerable changed my heart. For the first time in a very long career in international human rights advocacy, I saw people doing what I never imagined: they were putting their own lives on the line, literally, to save others from sexual assault and slavery. I saw a very long obedience to God among IJM's lawyers and social workers and investigators who worked for days, months, and years on behalf of a single prisoner or slave. They never gave up. Ever. I knew that the evil they stared down every day would have crushed me like an ant. It didn't crush them. I saw their joy in the midst of the ugliest things human beings can do to one another.

And I witnessed Gary and IJM's pastors spending every weekend preaching sermons at churches around the country. They told Christians about the issue I cared most about in life: violence against the poor. Their message was "God wants you to be involved." We can't go back and undo the Holocaust or the Rwanda genocide, but we can do something today about child prostitution, land grabs from widows, and police violence.

I didn't stop wondering why God permitted gross cruelty in the first place, and I don't understand it to this day. But IJM's theology of justice allowed me to imagine that God might possibly exist and that he could be good in a way I can only partially understand. Somehow, a cruel world and a good God no longer needed to be mutually exclusive concepts.

Gary and IJM showed what Jesus's command to "love your neighbor" looked like in real life. Our neighbor could be the seven-year-old Bolivian kid whose uncle has been raping him regularly, and the guy in an Indian rice mill working seventeen-hour days, along with his children, to pay off a fifty-dollar debt. As Gary put it, "What does love look like to that kid if nobody stops his abuser?

But the search for faith was an emotional journey as well as an intellectual one. My heart lagged well behind my head. I could at last believe that, in theory, God could be good and that the people who followed him could be too. But it didn't have meaning for my personal life for several years after hearing Gary's sermon. It would be hundreds of hours of conversation with my friend Sharon Cohn, with whom I was particularly close, before I would engage on all fronts.

I'd been slogging through a difficult patch of hyperanxiety, and I had come to the end of the line. That is, I'd come to the end of my wits, my cleverness, and my self-sufficiency. My brain was whirling with free-floating, irrational terror, and I couldn't do a thing about it.

I prayed for calm, and—mysteriously, stunningly, unexpectedly—that prayer was answered.

And thus I came to believe. Trust me, I'm still a left-wing feminist. And in many ways, I'm still a skeptic. That cry from Mark's gospel—"Lord, I believe. Help me in my unbelief"—is my cry too. And I am still on a desperate search for a loving God in a world of savagery and exploitation that hasn't changed much. Even though I have found God (or God has found me), the injustice that kept me from believing for so many decades is still the norm.

Because I believe now in a good God, I want to know where he—or she—is in a world that's still awful. So I decided to go back to those intellectual and spiritual boulders in the road that had blocked my path to God to see if the Creator might be somewhere in the midst of them. Thank heaven, there's help. Great minds have been chewing over the inequity of suffering, over despair and spiritual darkness, and over God's inscrutable tolerance of human cruelty since time began. Christian or non-Christian, agnostic or atheist, all of us have to wrestle with the reality and meaning of suffering, injustice, and degradation. No matter where you are on the road toward—or away from—faith, these questions matter deeply. They matter to the world, and they matter to our hearts and our lives.

I am not wise about God or faith or the Bible or loss and suffering. In fact, I am the clumsiest toddler among Christians. But after a lifetime of looking for a source of goodness in a world of cruelty, I stumbled across a good God in precisely the places I had cursed him for abandoning. And the more I saw of God's goodness, the more I came to *see*. Faith begat more faith, which begat more questions and more stumbling around while clutching my sippy cup.

In these pages I'm going to go back to the things that made me weep before I believed in God, and I'm going to try to see them through the lens of my newfound faith. I go searching through the mass murders, mental illnesses, land mines, and child rapes to see if there is evidence of a good God and to discern what he wants us to do. I wrestle with stories from the Bible that have always been the hardest for me to stomach, like the book of Job. And I try to make sense of loss and suffering in my own life.

All of this sounds pretty dreadful, doesn't it? I promise you, it's not. When I'm not obsessed with the Holocaust, I'm actually very funny. Hilarious, I like to think. I have a great life. I'm a highly energetic fifty-nine-year-old with dyed blond hair. (Don't judge!) I'm married to a kind, quiet man who puts up with a lot. John Fitzpatrick is a seventy-year-old university professor. He looks it. We are Grace and Josie's geezer parents. They're teenagers now and take very seriously the work of trying to make John and me modern. Just for laughs, you should also know I have heart disease, a colorful and checkered past, and just a smidge of mental illness.

I also have a job I love as a human rights activist at International Justice Mission. That's right, I hung around so long that eventually they hired me. I lead a team of extraordinary people young enough to be my kids, and they teach me every day what God's heart for justice looks like. For the record, while IJM has inspired much of my recent faith journey, the frequently ridiculous views I express in these pages are entirely my own.

Some wise person—I think it was me—said that it matters more in life what questions you ask than the answers you receive. Actually, a wise person (me again) said we need both. So let's do this thing. Let's go look for solutions to the toughest questions we *Homo sapiens* know how to ask. What is the meaning of suffering in the world, and what are we supposed to do about it?

The search itself has sharpened my eyes to see goodness and beauty all over the place that I had altogether missed before. I'm even taking a second look at that evangelical woman in West Africa who prayed for the tires on our Jeep and made me so furious those twenty-plus years ago. She was there with those terrified refugees and overflowing with joy at the honor of lending a hand to those whom God loves in this unkind world. I think that if we'd had a flat tire, she would have fallen to her knees in gratitude for the spare.

two

Adah, Unmoored

was born in 1954 and am told that I was a placid, happy, silent child. I had anemia as a toddler and would fall asleep wherever I happened to be, frequently on the landing of the staircase. There were five of us kids, nine years apart. The two older girls, Kathy and Karol, were followed by my brother, Gary; then came Roo and me. We had dark brown hair, dark brown eyes, and thick glasses for our poor vision—every one of us. We were extremely close-knit and always together.

Family lore has it that I didn't talk until I was five. That can't be right. My younger sister and best friend, Roo, and I were in constant communication; we just didn't talk to adults. When I did speak, Mom says my first words were "happy girl." Oh please. I'm sure I meant it ironically. Another data point was that I had an absurdly tender heart. In the 1950s my family would visit friends who had television. We didn't own a TV, so watching one was enchanting to my sisters and brother. My siblings would flop down on the floor in front of the box, chins propped on their elbows, eyes glued to the black-and-white set. But I would watch from the back of the room with my fingers over my eyes for fear that some animal would get hurt. And sure enough, a horse would inevitably fall down in some Western show, and I'd run away crying, to the smirks of my family.

As a quiet, timid little girl who hated conflict more than anything, I took on the job of trying to keep Roo out of trouble. She was a spunky, sassy little pea and vastly braver than I was. When she was scolded, she'd stick out her tongue and scream. Then she'd get into bigger trouble. I tried to school her in diplomacy, unsuccessfully.

We were quite poor in those days. My dad was working on his PhD at Ohio State University, and as a professional musician, he played viola jobs all over town. Our mother was at home until the youngest, Roo, went to kindergarten. Mom got her teaching certificate and taught seventh-grade English for a very long time thereafter. In the meantime, we bought our clothes from Goodwill and went to Dad's concerts for our birthdays. We didn't feel deprived—virtually everyone we knew in those years had big families and was poor.

Both my parents had been Mennonites; Dad's parents were missionaries in India for forty years. When I was little, a wealthy Presbyterian church in Columbus, Ohio, advertised a choir director position. It wasn't a Mennonite gig, but it was a paying gig for Dad. We became Presbyterians. I grew up in that church. My siblings and I sang in the kid choir or were ringers in the hand bell ensemble. Our family life revolved around church, religious holidays, and music. I don't remember a single sermon or scriptural passage in my ten years of perfect attendance at the Worthington Presbyterian Church. But I remember the choir. We knew every singer by name. We broke out in goose bumps when soprano Juanita Harrison sang solos and swelled with family esprit de corps when my father proceeded down the aisle and stood to conduct the anthem.

The church choir was also the Burkhalter family social life. Because we lived so frugally, choir parties were a big deal. There was a summer picnic where the dads and older kids took turns hand cranking the enormous ice cream barrel. Mother always made baked beans and her signature Lazy Daisy cake.

There were burgers on the grill and watermelon. We kids played badminton and ate as much cake and ice cream as we could hold. When the food was gone, the choir members wandered indoors to the piano and sang hymns in four-part harmony.

My father's shrine was music. He practiced violin and viola at home by the hour and played as many recordings as he and Mom could afford to buy. Mom and Dad would play classical LPs in the house, and we kids had a little record player that played 45s—salad-plate-sized discs of the classics: Mozart's *Eine kleine Nachtmusik,* Strauss waltzes, Haydn's *Trumpet Concerto.* We five Burkhalter children, when we were very young, played and danced to those records endlessly. To this day, when we hear a scrap of our childhood's soundtrack, we'll look at each other and say, "Little record."

Beautifully performed music was worship. Badly played music wasn't tolerated—it was virtually blasphemous. For most of my childhood, I didn't really distinguish between God and music. At our house, they were wholly intertwined.

When I was about eight, I got my first inkling that classical music sung superbly wasn't actually the answer to every problem. For weeks, my father had been talking to Mom about a problem in the choir while he drove us home after church. I listened from the backseat. A middle-aged woman— a resident at nearby Harding Hospital (a psychiatric hospital)—had joined the Worthington Presbyterian Church choir.

I saw her in the loft and could see that she was odd. My father knew that this woman desperately wanted to sing. But she sang badly, and the choir sound suffered. He wondered aloud what he should do. Because he was kind, he struggled for a solution.

As I sat in that car, I knew exactly what he should do and what he *would* do. It never occurred to me for one second that, at the end of the day, this woman wouldn't stay in the choir. She would sing; Dad would work it out. He was the epitome of goodness. The way was clear.

But it wasn't. My father asked her to leave, and I never saw her again. I struggled mightily to make sense of the paradox that what was good for the sick woman—singing—was bad for the choir. And conversely, what was good for the choir— that she leave—was bad for her. The incident didn't make me doubt God, but it made me very confused about having to choose between kindness and beautiful choral music.

The singer from Harding Hospital was my first experience, albeit peripheral, with mental illness, but it wasn't my parents'. My dad, as a pacifist Mennonite during World War II, was a conscientious objector. After they married, he and my mother worked as aides in two different mental institutions under the auspices of Civilian Public Service. For four years they witnessed appalling cruelties to adults with developmental and psychiatric disabilities who had been warehoused and forgotten in enormous state institutions. Dad used to say that the poorly paid, untrained hospital employees were sicker than the patients. The presence of Mennonites, Brethren, and Quakers in those institutions in the early 1940s led to a wave of reforms.

I didn't know it then, but both of my parents had family members with mental disabilities. Perhaps it is what drew them to work in those terrible institutions, as an expression of their Mennonite faith. Mental illness would wind through my own faith journey like a river.

When I was sixteen, I rejected God completely when my beloved grandmother had a mental breakdown.

Many Christians I know speak of experiencing God's presence as teenagers, and that cemented their faith for life. Not me. I experienced the reverse. I made a very deliberate decision that I did not believe in God. Or, to be more precise, I did not believe in a good God. It was when my grandmother, Adah Wenger, got sick.

When we were young and it was summer, my parents would drive Roo and me to Bluffton, Ohio, and leave us for a week with our grandparents, Adah and Paul Wenger. Those were the happiest days of my childhood. We played in the earth-smelling cellar that was lined with shelves of plump jars of home-canned peaches and green beans. Our grandmother taught us to make marigold garlands like she did in India, and we dressed up in saris for mint tea parties. Moss roses bloomed and sprawled from stone planters that rimmed the front porch, and the big bing cherry tree held us in its branches for hours.

We loved our grandmother's stories about her years in India as a missionary, especially those about "little Laurence," our dad. One day she gave me a big stack of her diaries to read. Her neat handwriting filled days and weeks and months with homey details of life in the compound and stories of friends, visitors, and of her son. But most entries were about her Christian faith—poems, prose, hymns.

I devoured each page, turning quickly to get to the next. Those first months in India in 1919 with her new missionary husband, Noah Burkhalter, were full of wonder and joy. The couple was immersed in Hindustani language study and settling in at the Mennonite compound in Janjgir.

And then the diary recorded the appalling news that Noah had contracted typhoid fever. After a four-week struggle, he died. Adah was six months pregnant.

As a kid, I asked my grandmother about it, and she described "darkness" after Noah's death. She didn't say so at the time, but I later learned that she experienced a mental breakdown and was virtually helpless for months. She credits a missionary friend, Elizabeth Penner, for bringing her through depression, pregnancy, and the birth of her son.

My dad's arrival gave Adah someone to love and respite

from her grief. She remained in India and six years later married a fellow missionary, Paul Wenger. She took his name, but her son kept his father's, Noah Laurence Burkhalter. Adah and Paul stayed in India until they retired from the mission field in 1955 and came home to America, retiring in the small town of Bluffton.

My father loved his stepfather, and so did we. He was everything a grandfather should be. In his retirement, Grandpa was the janitor at the Mennonite church. Nothing was finer than helping him dust the pews and empty the wastebaskets when I was little. My grandmother volunteered at a nearby nursing home, and Roo and I would visit our old lady friends there every day. It involved lots of hugs and candy and intense work on jigsaw puzzles in the day room.

When he was about seventy-five, my grandfather was diagnosed with prostate cancer, and his prospects were poor. At one point, a pastor was summoned to give him last rites, but the old man rallied. Against all odds, Grandpa Paul lived another seven years, and they were good years.

Cancer did catch up with my grandfather, though, and he died peacefully. But his death transformed my beautiful, brave grandmother. She was wholly deranged by her loss. I was shocked to see the long white hair that was usually in a neat bun now strewn over her shoulders. This once-dignified and competent woman was now hunched in a chair, weeping into her hands and incoherently calling on God. I heard her sob that God couldn't hear her and had abandoned her. My grandfather was gone, and God, to my horror and amazement, was gone as well. The Maker of the universe, the object of Adah's life of devotion and service, inscrutably declined to show up.

Listening to her terrible one-way conversations with God enraged me. "Where are you?" she pleaded. She prayed for a glimpse of God's presence, and that prayer was not answered. I concluded that it wasn't God's love that had sustained Adah all those years. No, it was her husband Noah's love first, and then Paul's. And as night follows day, their deaths, fifty years apart, unhinged her mind and her spirit.

God's absence when my grandfather died demolished my childish and puny faith. I flung it, and God, aside in disgust. I don't know if Adah lost her faith because she lost her mind, or if she lost her faith, which unbalanced her mind. But her suffering taught me three terrible lessons that I clung to for most of my adult life. Number one: God does not answer prayer. Number two: God is unavailable to the grief stricken and the mentally ill. And number three: a life of Christian faith and devotion was good for absolutely nothing when life fell apart.

How could I have believed otherwise? My grandmother was not only the kindest person I knew, she was also God's most obedient and faithful servant. It seemed inconceivable that the God she worshiped wouldn't show up when she needed him, but that's what I saw happen.

My grandmother suffered acute depression for about a

year. But she recovered her physical, spiritual, and mental health and moved to a Mennonite retirement community in Goshen, Indiana. There she lived and thrived for another twenty years, baking, gardening, walking, lecturing at the seminary, and writing poetry. No one's faith in God could have been more passionate and intelligent than Adah's when she was well.

But then the day came, for no reason that we knew, when my grandmother would get quieter and quieter. Her bright blue eyes would fill with tears, and she would bury her face in her hands, rocking and praying for God's comfort. She would stop talking and then stop eating. As Adah grew very aged, these episodes became more frequent and threatened her life. She was treated with electroconvulsive therapy—administered humanely—to disrupt whatever it was in her brain that was torturing her. It helped, for months or years, until the next attack would plunge her back into darkness.

I remember visiting my grandmother in the nursing home when she was suffering a period of acute depression. She was to undergo electroconvulsive therapy the next day, and she was incoherent with inexplicable grief and loss. I was at a loss myself, not knowing what to do for her. I just sat awkwardly by her side, with a present I'd brought on my lap. And then my grandmother did something so courageous and so kind that it rips my heart to remember it. She put aside her confusion and fear and offered me the only thing she had to make things easier. Summoning every ounce of mental strength, she said in a trembling voice, "We could open my present." So we did that. It was an alphabet wall hanging that I'd cross-stitched.

Soon they arrived to take her for treatment, and when she came back, she was calm again. Within a day, she could speak and eat normally. Whatever it was in her brain that had been terrorizing her was gone, for now.

We moved to Ames, Iowa, when Dad got a job in the music department at Iowa State University. Music and church continued to define my childhood. Since all of us Burkhalter kids played instruments, my father scored classical pieces for our peculiar family ensemble: Kathy and me on the piano, Roo and Karol on the violin, Gary on the cello, and of course my dad on the viola or violin. We actually performed in public on occasion, and I hated it passionately. Dad and my brother were naturals in front of an audience, but my sisters and I were scared stiff. I was so shy that performing was torture. But I lived in a family where performing was a way of life. Accordingly, I volunteered, insanely, for a vocal solo in my sixth-grade school-choir end-of-year performance. All I had to do was step forward at the end of the last song and sing this line: "Faraway places are calling." That's it: four words. I was so terrified that I stepped forward, opened my mouth, and absolutely no sound came out. Complete silence. I stood there in my new turquoise dress in front of my family and hundreds of others and sang nothing.

For a time, my father conducted the choir at the Presbyterian church a block from campus. Like almost everybody else in my junior high school, I was in the church youth group. It wasn't much for religious instruction, but my friends and I would sit around with some friendly young married couples and talk about Big Ideas. We teenagers would usually try to turn the conversation to sex. But the real purpose of the group was to wrangle us through the confirmation process.

I went through confirmation training along with twenty other eighth graders, but when the day came to actually say our vows in front of the congregation and participate for the first time in communion, I didn't do it. All my friends did, but I knew, dimly, that this was an important thing going on here. I knew that I didn't believe in any of it. God hadn't been real for my grandmother when she was ill, and God had never been real to me, and I thought it dishonest to pretend to have a faith I didn't understand or possess. I don't know if my opting out of confirmation and communion upset my parents. We didn't talk about it.

My brother's faith took an opposite turn. When he was a junior in high school, Gary joined a Campus Crusade for Christ chapter at the local Southern Baptist church. Campus Baptist was extremely conservative, socially and theologically.

The teens weren't allowed to go to school dances, and church-goers evangelized on the campus and at the state fair.

Now, if you want to poke my dad in the eye with a sharp stick, you couldn't do better than that. Notwithstanding our teetotaling background, my parents were definitely left of center in both theological and political terms. They were intellectual about their faith: our bookshelves sported C. S. Lewis, Dietrich Bonhoeffer, and Paul Tillich. Nothing was more repugnant to them than Christian fundamentalists who believed every word in the Bible was literally true.

Soon after joining the Baptists, my brother was asked to play the cello at his new church. He invited us to come. The whole family trudged in and filled up a pew near the front. As usual, music still trumped everything. If Gary was going to play, we were going to be there. The pastor introduced my brother with these words: "This is Brother Gary. He was saved recently." At that precise moment, my father, who was so tense he could hardly sit still, broke in half the pencil he'd been clutching. He'd raised his son as a Christian, not a fundamentalist. "Brother" and "saved" weren't part of the Burkhalter religious vernacular.

Gary's conversion and conservative theology were anathema to the rest of the family. But ultimately it was politics that estranged us from Christianity, as it did for virtually every other liberal I knew. Jerry Falwell founded the Moral Majority in 1979, and the politics of abortion, creationism, and prayer in public schools exploded onto the national agenda. As my brother became more religious and more conservative, his sisters and parents became less religious and more liberal.

It's weird. When we were children, nobody ever announced that they were a Christian. Nobody needed to. Where I grew up in the Midwest, there was no one who *wasn't* a Christian. But the cultural and social changes of the 1960s and 1970s and my cynicism about God, based on my grandmother's suffering, demolished whatever lingering respect I had for Christianity. By the time I finished college and moved to Washington to work for Congress in 1979, I had come to believe that Christians were, in the main, book-banning, anti-intellectual, exclusive bigots.

Other than that, I'm sure they were very nice.

three

Behold, I Have Two Daughters

I have always objected to exclusivity in any form, and it feels particularly irksome and annoying when it comes from those who claim to represent a God of love. But exclusivity on the part of Christians is hardly new and isn't limited to the right-wing evangelicals, whose voices I heard loudest before my faith journey began. There's an old joke about some newly arrived folks on a tour of heaven. The angel takes them by a door marked Methodists and another labeled Baptists. But he instructs them to tiptoe past the door marked Catholics. Why? Because they think they're the only ones here. I'm sure nearly every denomination has its own variation of this joke, and someone else is always the punch line.

Several years ago the Evangelical Lutheran Church in America was fractured over the question of gay people in the clergy. My brother, Gary, now an ordained Lutheran pastor, joined the conservative breakaway group, which is now known as the North American Lutheran Church. When Gary's wife, Betty, and I talked about the schism, she said, "Well, it's not your church. You don't have any stake in it. You guys should go work on your own churches."

Tim Keller, pastor of Redeemer Presbyterian Church in Manhattan, put it this way: "Any community that did not hold its members accountable for specific beliefs and practices would have no corporate identity and would not really be a community at all."

It's a fair point. Every single organization of human beings defines itself and its membership in some way or other. But the process of self-definition invariably becomes a process of excluding. Roman Catholics won't even serve communion to divorcées and non-Catholics. Many Protestant churches, and of course the Catholic Church, prohibit women in the clergy. Most churches require that members formally adopt a set of theological beliefs that, to my eyes, goes well beyond anything Jesus asked, which was "Follow me."

Before I became a Christian myself, I didn't know what Jesus asked and I didn't want to know. I did, however, know way too much about what churches were requiring, and because I didn't distinguish between God and those channeling for him, I wanted no part of it.

It's too bad that I let said Christians do my thinking for me. I didn't know about Jesus's passionate love for the sick, deranged, poor, despised, and degraded. Theologian Robin Meyers wrote about Jesus and his disciples' "radical hospitality" to people who were different. He recalled the story of an Ethiopian eunuch who met Jesus's disciple Philip.

> Philip expounds on the meaning of the life of Jesus, and the eunuch recognizes that the prophet speaks to him—even to *him*, who bears a stigmatizing mark and will never have children. At that moment, he asks the most urgent question of our time when it comes to all those who have been left out: "What is to prevent me from being baptized?" The answer is *nothing*.

Some churches are like that in our time, but I didn't know them. What I saw were church leaders dividing up Christendom, splitting into ever-smaller denominations and drawing circles around themselves that explicitly excluded others. It makes me mad when I see Christians doing things that seem to bear no resemblance to Jesus's and the disciples' extraordinary inclusiveness.

There was a disgraceful episode of this following the massacre of schoolchildren at Sandy Hook in December 2012. Rev. Rob Morris, a Lutheran pastor in the town of Newtown, Connecticut, gave the benediction for a prayer service for the victims. President Obama and others attended the interfaith service, which included various Christian denominations as well as Muslims and Baha'is. Several days later, the leadership of Rev. Morris's Lutheran denomination, the Lutheran Church–Missouri Synod, stepped forward and publicly rebuked him for participating. He apologized.

At a time when the whole nation was looking for hope and comfort, a church rebuking its pastor for praying at a community event didn't just make the Missouri Synod look bad. For nonbelievers and skeptics, it made God look bad as well. Who wants to be part of a faith that produces *that*?

I didn't read much of the Bible during my childhood and almost none throughout most of my adulthood. I glanced at it now and then, but there are too many stories in it that made no sense to me. I would either get tangled up in chapters of detail about animal sacrifice or dietary law in Leviticus or infuriated by God destroying Egyptian baby boys in Exodus. I didn't try to understand or ask biblically literate people to help me, because I didn't really want to learn. God's heart for the widow and the orphan came to me later—when I met IJM. In the meantime there was Job.

Job is a major character in the Old Testament. His tribulations are so famous that his name is virtually a synonym for gratuitous suffering. Extermination of his every child. Loss of his livelihood. Drought. Locusts. Boils. Degradation. Despair. Scraping oozing sores with chunks of broken pottery.

Theologian C. S. Lewis said that even the difficult parts of the Bible are there "for our learning." What can we learn from the book of the Bible that asks the hardest question in the universe: Why do bad things happen to good people?

As the story goes, God and the devil argue over the pious and honorable Job. The devil says that Job only believes because he's had a good life. God invites the devil to test Job, and there follows a tidal wave of suffering, death, illness, and isolation. Job is forgotten by his brothers and friends, his wife is repulsed, and even young children loathe him. Job pleads, "Have pity on me, have pity on me, O you my friends, for the hand of God has touched me! Why do you, like God, pursue me?"

Notwithstanding the losses of every kind that he has suffered, Job knows he is good and is confident that, if he could make his case to God, he will be believed. He finally gets his chance. He puts the question to God, which is everyman's question, forever and ever, amen: "Why are you doing terrible things to me?" God's answer is quite horrible. Put simply, it is "Because I can." For the next hundred verses, God describes himself as the Creator of the universe and reminds Job of his smallness. And that's his answer. There isn't anything else, other than God occasionally tweaking Job, with the question "Can you do that?" whether it's causing the sun to rise or dragging a sea monster around on a leash.

At the end of God's oration, Job is forced to concede God's superiority, and he concludes that the reason why he was singled out for unrelenting atrocities is a mystery. But then it seems that God himself repents of the trials he inflicted, because the Bible reports that he restores many times over what was taken away from Job. He even gets replacement children, though not, regrettably, a nicer wife.

Why, you ask, did I go looking for a good God in the book of Job, of all places? I had read it before I believed in God, and I've read it many times since because it is the place in Scripture where the question of why God permits suffering is explored the most fully. Job's question is my question and yours and Aquinas's and Pascal's. It is the question that I most want an answer to. But I don't like the answer we get from Job's God. The answer to why God inflicted suffering on Job was "I did it because I'm powerful and you're not."

Well this is a fine how-de-do. This is why the Bible made me so mad before I became a Christian—and still does. Recently, I beetled off to ask my friend and colleague Eileen, who went to Harvard Divinity School and knows Things. I threw Job at her and demanded an explanation for how the God of Love turns into the God of Cruelty in the book of Job.

To my astonishment, Eileen said that Job is her favorite book of the Bible. And why is that? "Because for the first time, illness is de-coupled from sin in the Bible." Trust Eileen, a longtime HIV/AIDS treatment activist, to come up with that. It's a cool way to think about Job and offers me a welcome alternative to the image of God tormenting one of his creatures at the suggestion of the devil just for the heck of it. The Job story makes it plain that good or bad doesn't make any difference in terms of loss and suffering. Nobody gets out of this life alive, including the decent, generous, kindly, and upright.

This view has marvelous ramifications about how we think of illness. In Job's day and well into our own time, illness, misfortune, and poverty are assumed to be consequences of sin. But the book of Job offers a resounding *no* to all that. There was absolutely nothing that Job could have done to prevent the loss of his family, crops, animals, and health. He was a good and upright man who suffered through no fault of his own.

That's the good news from Job: having phenomenally bad luck doesn't mean you're a sinner. The bad news is that awful things happen to good people. Both true. But can it really be true that God actually orchestrated the death of Job's children and the destruction of his health and fortune?

And if God tortured Job, did he set the Holocaust in motion? As an atheist, I shouldn't have cared what the book of Job had to say on the matter. But I did care. I was that weird nonbeliever who actually wanted to believe in a good God.

Over the years of my disbelief, I had plenty of ammunition against the concept of a good God from the Bible itself, but my strongest defense against faith in a good God was all the unchecked brutality around the world. I was very familiar with atrocities. I didn't believe in God, but I did believe in *us*—my smart, hard-driving, passionate friends and colleagues in the international human rights movement. And then there was the Rwanda genocide, and by the end of it I had stopped believing in us as well.

I had a personal connection to the Rwanda genocide through my friend and colleague Alison Des Forges. She was my favorite activist of them all. Tiny, gray-haired, sweet-voiced, and fiercely intelligent, Alison knew months before the butchery started that something was wrong. It was January 1994, and she was reading a letter from a friend, a Rwandan Catholic priest. He wrote, "Why are Tutsis being murdered in my parish?" Alison began collecting and disseminating information about sporadic killings around the country—four here, ten there—and demanded that Rwanda's government, its foreign donors, and the United Nations stop them.

Four months later, Hutu extremists activated the campaign of Tutsi slaughter they had rehearsed with the earlier killings. As each demonic stage of the genocide unfolded, Alison, who was Human Rights Watch's Rwanda expert, worked harder and longer. It must have been hell for her. Her Tutsi friends in Kigali were in hiding, and they would call her at our office in Washington, begging to know how long before UN peacekeepers would secure the city and save them. One by one, those calls stopped coming. Her friends and their children had been found and butchered, to the last tiny baby who was thrown alive into a well. Help never came.

I was desperately bitter about that. I cursed God day after day, but why? I didn't believe in God, so why did I feel that he had betrayed Rwanda? I must have had some shred of hope that he or those who believed in him would throw a life preserver into the carnage. I was infuriated by a passive, uncaring Creator and outraged by Christians who *did* believe. How dare they believe in a good God, or a strong God, or God at all?

Old Testament stories don't provide the answer. The book of 1 Samuel reports that God ordered Saul, the Israelite commander, to wipe out every breathing creature in Amalek: "Now go and attack Amalek, and utterly destroy all that they have; do not spare them, but kill both man and woman, child and infant, ox and sheep, camel and donkey." Under God's approving eye, Israelite commanders slaughtered unarmed people, from infants to grandparents, with efficiency. Food stores were set aflame, women were taken as slaves. Defeated and wounded soldiers who had dropped their weapons were murdered where they lay.

The God of the Old Testament promised to protect his people, sure, but he also managed to wipe out creation with an epic flood, blow up Sodom and Gomorrah, and butcher a generation of Egyptian baby boys. Why would this God do something for Rwanda in 1994?

If you take these stories literally, the Old Testament's warrior God who swooped down to kill Israel's enemies was a mass murderer. When I was a nonbeliever, I found such stories repulsive. Today, as a Christian, I simply don't believe them.

There's really only one way for me to reconcile a good God with the Rwanda genocide, and that is to take literally some *other* words of the Bible, like these from Hebrews 13: "Remember those who are in prison, as though you were in prison with them; those who are being tortured, as though you yourselves were being tortured." It is life's great mystery why God wants the work of justice on this earth to be done by his people. To be honest, I'd prefer something faster and more reliable than stupid, blundering *us,* but that's what we've got. That's what I learned from Gary Haugen's sermon ten years after the genocide, and now I believe him.

So let's not ask where God was when the balloon went up in Kigali in April 1994. Let's ask where God's people were. And here is what I learned. Many Christians in Rwanda were actually complicit in the genocide. The churches, to which tens of thousands of terrified Tutsi Rwandans fled, became slaughterhouses. Some researchers believe that more people were murdered in churches than in any other location in Rwanda. And Rwanda's church leadership refused to condemn the killing—even on church property. Hutu clergy killed Tutsi priests and nuns. And worldwide, Christendom was virtually silent.

And so were we all. After the genocide, I asked a senior US policymaker why President Clinton had refused to send a small US force to stop the genocide. The ambassador, a friend of mine, said, "Because the American people did not demand it." And that is true. There was no groundswell against the genocide among American Christians or among anybody else.

But there was Alison. Alison, who never gave up hoping that our government and others would change course and stop the genocide. Alison, who wrote the epic human rights report "Leave None to Tell the Story," which captures all we should know about the genocide. It honors those who stood up to the *génocidaires,* defended the victims, and died with them. It remembers the hundreds of thousands of dead, and most important of all it tells us very thoroughly and scrupulously what the world might have done to prevent and stop the slaughter. Alison Des Forges couldn't do it herself—we needed armies for that—but she walked through the valley of the shadow of death and left it better for having been there.

And what I believe now is that God was wherever Alison

was during the genocide. She was the perfect picture of love for the poor and the abused. She fought for them. She shamed the world for abandoning them, and she never stopped believing that things didn't have to be this way. She was the antigenocide. It was what Jesus would have been like if he had been here in April 1994.

I saw in those appalling days and weeks some extraordinary goodness and courage in Alison that went well beyond anything I had ever experienced. Her work and friendship and witness to sufferers of genocide showed me how truly great human beings can be, right in the midst of when they were at their worst.

And though I did not believe in God at that time—and I don't know if she did—Alison was crucial to my faith journey: she made it absolutely, indisputably clear that *people* were responsible for the genocide. She named them and testified against them in eleven genocide cases before the International Criminal Tribunal for Rwanda, and she captured their crimes for all to remember. Deep in my cynical heart, I blamed God. But God didn't murder eight hundred thousand Rwandans. As Alison insisted, the mass killings were the result of human choices. Choices by Rwandans, including significant elements of the Catholic and Anglican churches, and choices by Americans, Europeans, and Africans to turn aside and let Rwanda die.

Alison Des Forges was killed on February 12, 2009, when

her commuter flight crashed as it approached her hometown of Buffalo. She was returning from her good, good work at Human Rights Watch in New York City.

I didn't believe then, like I do now, that Alison served as God's hands and feet in Rwanda. I just knew that the mission had failed and my confidence in human rights advocacy had been broken. Then a different kind of atrocity finally broke my heart.

It was early 2003 when Sharon Cohn of IJM came to my office at Physicians for Human Rights with a piece of undercover video from Cambodia. Sharon and I had become friends when she joined IJM a year earlier. She led IJM's overseas work and spent months in the field, gathering evidence of crimes against children. I invited some human rights experts to meet with her and advise IJM about what to do about Cambodia.

The jerky, grainy, black-and-white film was taken with a hidden camera by an IJM investigator posing as a Western pedophile. In the course of a three-week investigation in the brothel neighborhood of Svay Pak, Cambodia, IJM's undercover agents had gathered data on dozens of minor girls being offered for sexual acts.

The video showed a crowd of young girls, approximately five to ten years of age, and a brothel owner answering questions about what sexual acts they would perform. All of them were Vietnamese—trafficked into Cambodia or sold there by their parents. Their pimp offered them for oral sex, which he called "yum yum," for thirty dollars. One child named Linh was so small that the other girls held her up in their arms to the supposed customer, the IJM investigator.

These girls were really little. I knew exactly how little they were. Our own daughter Josie is Vietnamese; we adopted her as an infant. She was five years old when I saw that video, the same age as little Linh in the film. My Josie weighed thirty pounds, and I still liked to carry her around on my hip, with her bony little arms wound around my neck. She could have been one of the girls in the undercover video.

When Sharon showed me the film, those little girls were still in prostitution. IJM had taken the video and other evidence to the Cambodian authorities, who said thank you very much and then proceeded to do absolutely nothing. It was only when the newly appointed US ambassador to Cambodia, Charles Ray, viewed IJM's evidence that things started to change.

Ambassador Ray went to the top of the Cambodian government. He contacted the deputy prime minister and led him to understand that a significant portion of US foreign assistance to Cambodia would be withdrawn if authorities failed to eradicate child sexual exploitation. IJM trained a unit of the Phnom Penh police and arranged a sting operation to retrieve the children and apprehend the perpetrators.

Plan A was for the pimps to bring the little girls to a hotel for a supposed sex party with IJM's operatives, posing as pedophile customers. At the last minute there was a tip-off. The brothel owners and traffickers refused to part with the girls and demanded that the customers have their party in the brothels. The team executed Plan B: Cambodian police broke down the doors of the brothels and brought thirty-five minor girls out of Svay Pak. Ten of them were under ten years of age; the youngest was five. One seven-year-old had been in the brothel since she was four.

I was overjoyed to learn about the rescues. Then I learned that not all of the girls in the video had been found. Little Linh, the five-year-old in the undercover video, wasn't in the brothels at the time of the sting, nor were five of the other little girls previously identified by our investigators.

Getting close to individual victims is costly. Every person who serves the poor and the abused and the hungry has to live in the horrifying knowledge that there are many just like them whose names we don't know. Those unknown victims will be raped or starved or endure humiliation and pain, and there will be no one to hear them crying.

A couple of decades ago, South African journalist Kevin Carter took a very important picture. It is a picture of a starving Sudanese toddler. She is alone and naked but for a silver necklace and bracelet, and her pipe-cleaner legs are folded under her. She has crawled and collapsed; her head is in her tiny hands. Two yards away sits a vulture, waiting patiently for a meal.

That famine claimed hundreds of thousands of lives, but it was the picture of one little girl that made it unbearable to the world. Public anguish over the toddler was so overwhelming that the London *Times* later reported that she had made it to a feeding center after Mr. Carter shooed away the vulture. Money for famine relief poured in. Kevin Carter won the Pulitzer Prize for the photo.

Two months later Kevin Carter killed himself by inhaling carbon monoxide from the exhaust pipe of a truck. He wrote, "I am depressed…I am haunted by the vivid memories of killings and corpses and anger and pain…of starving or wounded children, of trigger-happy madmen, often police, of killer executioners."

Kevin Carter and the vultures, the starving toddler and little Linh—I could not bear it. Who can? The complete randomness of some girls getting to live in freedom and others to be raped until they died, the randomness of one toddler crawling to the refugee camps and thousands of others dying in the dust was a devastating indictment of God. If I had believed. But in those days and years I didn't believe, and the world was a horror show.

four

Squirming in My Seat

had lots of reasons not to believe in God: Misery in the world. My grandmother's mental illness. An Old Testament God who was mean and punishing. Judgmental and sanctimonious Christians. The poisonous synergies between right-wing politics and religious fundamentalism.

On the other hand, I also had many

reasons to believe in God: My family's deep roots in the Mennonite church. My grandparents' life as missionaries. My brother's happiness in his late-in-life ordination as a pastor. IJM's sturdy obedience to God's commandments to rescue widows, orphans, and prisoners. My new Christian friends in the human rights field.

It would be so glorious to pinpoint the place where my reasons to believe overwhelmed my reasons not to. As hard-headed and skeptical as I am, God should have whipped me to the ground and stomped on my spine to get my attention like he did the apostle Paul. I wish I could name and treasure that moment of amazing grace, when once I was blind but now I see.

That was the kind of experience my friend Oil Tanchan-pong had when she came to faith. Oil (pronounced *Oy*) works for IJM in Thailand. We went shopping together at the end of a week-long staff training up in Chiang Mai. Taking a break to swig down a couple of cans of Thai iced coffee, Oil talked about how she came to be a Christian. The daughter of Buddhists, Oil had left Thailand in her twenties to attend college in Seattle. An American friend told her that the God who made the birds and flowers made her also. Oil liked that. She joined a Bible study group and stayed on in the United States for another two years to study Christianity.

At this point in her story, I'm thinking, *Well, dang it! How come Oil gets to glide into faith on the strength of birds and flow-*

ers, and I have to struggle for about forty years? But there was more to Oil's story. She said she really came to believe in God because he worked a miracle in her life.

Oil had been helping a fellow student at the university with his schoolwork. She had stayed up most of the night working on the paper for him, and in the morning she didn't feel good about it. She put the question to God: *God, if you love me, please tell me if this is a good man.* Then she put the document on a disk and went to class.

When Oil's friend tried to open the document, he simply couldn't. Oil bought a new disk, returned to her computer, downloaded the assignment, and returned it to him. Nothing. Exasperated, she took both disks to her sister's office and slipped them into a fancy new computer. The screen promptly lit up with the news that her document had been destroyed. That was that. The guy was history, and Oil believed in God.

Now that's what I call a sign. My own faith journey was different. I didn't believe in God for almost forty years, and now I do. But there was a period of time when, without my knowing it, I was moving closer to believing. I was transitioning into faith. It took a long time.

Becoming a parent and experiencing unbounded, unconditional love for our daughters was the beginning. I never knew it was possible to love like that, and I dimly understood that there must be a source for that love other than my own feeble heart. It wasn't Jesus I'd fallen in love with; it was Grace and Josie, but the first footprints of a journey to faith began with them.

Simultaneously my intellectual fire wall against Christianity gradually eroded, largely because of my relationships with Christians I admired intensely. I began to imagine that God might be good and might be real, even if not to me. I met such a Christian in 2001. That was the year that the organization I then worked for, Physicians for Human Rights, held a meeting of the International Campaign to Ban Landmines. We invited two hundred activists to Washington for the third anniversary of the historic anti-mine treaty's signing.

If ever there were evidence of an indifferent God, the scourge of antipersonnel land mines was it. So many broken, maimed, blinded, amputated scraps of humanity strewn across the globe. It was as if some gigantic, deranged child threw millions of his dolls into a blender and switched it to chop. I raged against those vile weapons in those days. I raged against the soldiers who left them behind after the wars were over. I raged against the gutless politicians who opposed the mine ban treaty. And, in my heart, I raged against an uncaring God in a world that is rigged against the poor and the young and the disabled.

Several dozen of those who came to the conference to ban land mines were land mine survivors themselves. Those heroes—missing legs, arms, or eyes—were the sturdiest proponents of the global mine ban treaty. They were the wind under the campaign's wings. One of them was Margaret, a beautiful Ugandan mother. Margaret had been on a bus, returning home from work, when it was ambushed by Ugandan rebel forces known as the Lord's Resistance Army (LRA). The fighters pulled women and girls off the bus and raped them. To escape, Margaret scrambled off the road into the bush. She stepped on an antipersonnel mine; it tore off her leg.

When I met Margaret, she had been living with the injury for less than a year, and the stump was badly infected. She was our keynote speaker for a major event in the conference, but the night before her speech, she was in terrible pain and burning with fever.

Happily, we knew just the person to help Margaret. I called Dr. Jim Cobey at home, and he came directly to the hotel to see her. Jim has had a lot of experience with land mine victims. He doesn't see many in his Washington orthopedic surgical practice, but he has logged months of his vacation time in countries riddled with antipersonnel land mines. He teaches local doctors how to amputate ruined limbs and save lives.

When Jim got a look at Margaret's injury, he said, "She'll have to come into the hospital right now." He made sure we knew he'd take care of all the arrangements and costs. But Margaret—sick, frightened, and very far from home—flatly refused. So Jim stayed right there in her room, cleaned her wound, and gave her a powerful blast of intravenous antibiotic. Within twelve hours she was at the podium, speaking to hundreds of anti–land mine activists.

Margaret spoke about her injury and the horrors of the weapon that at that time was still buried by the millions in sixty countries. Some had been newly planted, but many were decades old, still lurking beneath the soil after conflicts had ended and the soldiers had gone home. Here's the deal: there are two methods for removing land mines. You can scientifically locate them with metal detectors, bomb-sniffing dogs, and heavily protected mine removal experts combing through every inch of suspected soil. Or you can leave the mines in the ground where children go out to play, old women fetch water, and goats graze. They won't even have to look—all they have to do is step on the ground the mines are buried beneath and the weapon will find them.

That is what had happened to Margaret. But even more dramatic than Margaret's story was the point in her speech when she thanked God for her amputation. She said she experienced Jesus's presence much more after her injury, that he had blessed her daily with love and friends and had given her good work to do in helping other land mine survivors.

I squirmed in my seat. I was not a believer, and neither were the vast majority of the American and European conference participants. I hadn't expected them to be subjected to a sermon! But my discomfort shamed me. This was Margaret!

I'd been with her all night long while she fought infection, fever, vomiting, and horrendous pain so that she could be on that stage. I thought, *Okay, I love her, but she's a religious nut.* But I knew in my heart she wasn't a nut at all. She was a powerful and gracious woman who spoke with absolute conviction. She really meant what she said about her suffering and her service to others making her a better person.

Margaret might not have been God's first messenger to me, but she's the first one I heard. Her radiant faith in God—which grew in her suffering—was a complete contradiction to my own notions about faith. Throughout most of my adult life, I strongly believed there was no integrity to believing in God if one had been blessed in life as richly as I had. Who *wouldn't* believe in a good God if they had health, a lovely roof over their head, great family, and so forth?

I stubbornly refused to find God in my blessings so long as there were those who had none such. Every single time my heart yearned to thank the Creator of pink skies, cookies, my daughters, and Handel's *Messiah,* I fiercely yanked it back into line. That's cheap grace for the privileged, and I was having none of it. The real test of God would be his faithfulness to the poor and abused and abandoned, those who had precious little reason to sing the "Hallelujah Chorus."

Charles Dickens has a character in his great novels named Mark Tapley. Mark subscribes to a hilarious variant of my disbelief in God. While I refused to believe in a good God so long as there were people hungrier, sadder, sicker, and poorer than I was, Mark Tapley refused to believe in his own goodness and generosity unless it made him miserable.

The novel is *Martin Chuzzlewit,* and Mark is a genial young pub attendant at the Blue Dragon. Tapley isn't the brightest bulb in the chandelier, but he's generous and kind, in contrast to the book's selfish and whiney hero, Martin Chuzzlewit himself. Tapley signs up to be Martin's servant, and the pair sets off to see the world.

As Martin seeks his fortune, Mark has another quest in mind. It is his life's ambition to do some good in the world that does not gratify him personally. Everywhere he goes, he lends a hand to people in desperate straits, but his pleasure in their affection for him cancels out his good deeds. Accordingly, he resolves to leave his beloved pub and look for something dreary.

When the two sail to America, Mark makes himself useful everywhere among the poorest passengers who suffer appallingly in steerage. He gives away his coat and blankets, bathes children, dispenses grog, and sings off-color songs. "In short, there never was a more popular character than Mark Tapley...and he attained at last to such a pitch of universal admiration that he began to have grave doubts within himself whether a man might reasonably claim any credit for being jolly under such exciting circumstances."

As Tapley puts it, "I never *am* to get any credit, I think. I begin to be afraid that the Fates is determined to make the world easy to me."

I felt like the world had been pretty easy to me too. Unlike Mark, who entered joyfully into others' pain to hand around hot alcoholic beverages, I felt guilty about joy because there were others who lacked it. But I have learned to accept what Ann Voskamp wrote in *One Thousand Gifts:*

> Rejecting joy to stand in solidarity with the suffering doesn't rescue the suffering. The converse does. The brave who focus on all things good and all things beautiful and all things true, even in the small, who give thanks for it and discover joy even in the here and now, they are the change agents who bring fullest Light to all the world.

Some years after meeting Margaret at the land mines conference, I met two more Christians who, like Margaret, exemplified Voskamp's change agents. Their thinking and values and work were so admirable and their lives so joyful that my un-faith narrative crumbled a little more. I came away thinking, *How do I get to be like them?*

It was early 2006, and Physicians for Human Rights convened a meeting of Christian health professionals to discuss best practices in the treatment and prevention of HIV/AIDS. It was an unprecedented event for the secular organization, but

PHR hoped the group could help bridge the gap between conservative Christian values and effective health practice, especially on the question of condom use to prevent AIDS transmission. Our conferees were Bible-believing doctors and nurses who saw no contradiction whatsoever between biblical truth and medical professionalism. For their patients—homosexual men, women with multiple partners, intravenous drug users—condoms were essential to prevent HIV transmission.

The Roman Catholic bishop of Rustenburg, South Africa, was the keynote speaker. Bishop Kevin Dowling is the only one of Africa's thirty Roman Catholic bishops to publicly and purposefully confront his church's official doctrine on condoms. Kevin's interpretation of Catholic theology is that condoms' prevention of conception is a "lesser evil" than exposure to HIV from unprotected sex. Thus condom use is not only justified but morally imperative. In his words, "The use of a condom can be seen not as a means to prevent the 'transmission of life' leading to pregnancy, but rather as a means to prevent the 'transmission of death' to another."

When asked by a reporter what advice he would give to the pope, Bishop Kevin reiterated his strong support for the Catholic values of abstention before marriage and fidelity after. But he said that the church required a different approach for desperately poor women who are engaging in "survival sex" just to make enough money for a meal. Here are his words:

I've sat with vulnerable women for years in their
shacks, have seen them and the babies in their arms
dying of AIDS. Their hopelessness has seared my heart
and spirit. I believe Jesus's injunction to the Pharisees
applies to me. He said that they are the ones who put
impossible burdens on the shoulders of their people but
will they lift a finger to help them carry them? Not
they. I want to be the one who lifts a finger.

Bishop Kevin is a courageous man and a hero to HIV/
AIDS activists. I expected to admire him greatly for his work,
but after spending a few days with him, I admired him most
for who he is. Kevin is a very calm, loving man. When he
talked with me and others, he was completely present. The
only word I can think of to describe him is *joyful*. As the bishop
of a poor diocese that has one of the highest rates of HIV
prevalence in the world, Kevin is neck deep in suffering and
death and hopelessness. But he might be the most peaceful,
happy man I have ever met.

My friend Eileen asked Kevin what keeps him going. He
thought a bit and said, "I had a serious illness several years ago
caused by stress. I almost died. That's when I realized I would
have to change to live. Centering prayer is what balances my
life. And my two dogs. I learned about the Lord's unconditional love from my dogs."

How about that? While Kevin Dowling's dogs are channeling God's love to him, he is channeling it to destitute women and kids in a South African slum. It takes the form of love, songs, antiretroviral drugs, jobs, and condoms for impoverished women in prostitution. He places infinite value on each of the broken and beaten and sick who crosses his path. He served them until he got very sick himself. His dogs helped make him well.

Unconditional love from God, dogs, and a bishop. Awesome.

five

The Noise in My Brain

Becky Kuhn was at the same HIV/AIDS conference that Bishop Kevin Dowling attended. Becky is an HIV/AIDS doctor in California. Most of her patients are IV drug users or gay men or both. Like Kevin, she's an extraordinary professional. But it was her warmth and sweetness that made the biggest impression on me. Because I met the two of them just as I was coming to faith, I think of Kevin Dowling and Becky Kuhn as those angels at the very end of a marathon who pass water bottles and snacks to people who are dropping from exhaustion as they approach the finish line.

Becky and I talked throughout the conference and afterward about how she deals with her patients' illness and their life-threatening behaviors, as a physician and an evangelical Christian. She said a wondrous thing that I carried around with me for years after meeting her, turning it over in my mind like a talisman: "I had to meet my patients on the path they were on and love them there, just as they were, before I could convince them to protect themselves, their health, and their partners."

In Becky's experience, her skill as a doctor is necessary but not sufficient to fully *heal*. She also has to love unconditionally. As a matter of fact, she can't even get to the point where people in desperate need can be treated unless she first meets them where they are and loves them. This is a radical concept for a healthcare professional. As a matter of fact, it's a radical concept for any of us.

I thought about Becky so many times when I was transitioning to faith. That notion of loving people exactly as they are—loving them without requiring them to earn it or to change or improve. It is a perfect description of Jesus's unconditional love, and I heard it first from her.

I phoned her some years after we met to capture some of

that first conversation that meant so much to me. She told me about her practice as a physician and a Christian. In describing her first conversations with new HIV/AIDS patients, Becky said, "I create a no-penalty zone where people can lay down their defenses and identify what they are afraid of. And they are all afraid of the same thing. Every one of my patients—pedophiles, crack whores, right-wing evangelicals, and secretaries using crystal meth—all have the same longing: Don't lie to me. Don't leave me." She went on to say, "That fear lives in me too. I can meet them there on that road."

In our conversation, Becky transitioned from talking about health to talking about the church. "The church should be a place where people can come and be loved, particularly in their brokenness, failure, and suffering. It should be that no-penalty zone where you don't get lied to and you don't get left."

That got my defenses against Christianity really crumbling. I had met three deeply faithful people: a Ugandan land mine survivor, a Roman Catholic bishop, and a heart-on-her-sleeve evangelical doctor. They were spending their lives entering into others' suffering, and they believed that is the great and good mission of the Christian church.

The evidence for a kind God in a crappy world was accumulating steadily. I wanted so badly to believe because I wanted that joy and calm and purpose that were so visible in Margaret, Bishop Kevin, and Becky, but I still didn't sense God's presence in my life in the way that he clearly was in theirs. It was prayer, in the end, that brought me to faith. My first prayers grew out of conversations I had been having with Sharon, my IJM friend. We saw each other often, mostly to walk around Capitol Hill, where we both lived, and drink coffee and talk.

I'm very liberal and Sharon isn't, so sometimes I'd fire questions at her about Christians, the Bible, and social and political issues we disagreed on. But mostly we talked about our lives. We talked about our siblings and parents, about losses and reboots. We talked about what's hilarious in everyday life and made each other hoot with laughter.

Sharon is extremely smart, which instantly deprived me of one of my best defenses against Christianity: that Christians are just a bit denser than the rest of us and need a helping hand to figure it all out. Sharon had the fiercest intellect I'd ever encountered, and she applied it directly to the question of whether God was real. If Sharon had actually set about converting me, it would have been a short conversation. Or if she'd had that fatuous certainty I associated with believers of any stripe. Or if she hadn't been so honest about the potholes and land mines on her spiritual road, or hadn't been so hilarious about it.

But the greatest gift to me on my journey was simply the way Sharon was. In those early days at IJM, Sharon headed up all the overseas work and traveled constantly to the organization's field offices. She led our national teams as they walked alongside local police to rescue enslaved families from brick kilns in India and girls from brothels. She interviewed children who had been raped by trusted relatives, and she sat beside a little client as she lay in a hospital bed, dying of AIDS.

Just after returning from one trip to Kolkata, Sharon told me about walking through a red-light district. She stopped to talk to a beautiful young girl, probably about thirteen or fourteen years old. While they chatted, a customer twenty years older than the child came up to them and pulled out his wallet. She watched as he led her away to be raped.

I dimly saw that it was costly for Sharon to be so close to evil and suffering. She would be very quiet when she first returned from the field. And then she would be back at work and within weeks on a plane to help IJM's teams in the field to investigate crimes against widows and children and slaves.

I talked to Sharon a lot about the costs and sorrows of human rights work. We talked, too, about my own increasing hyperactivity and anxiety. For much of my life, I have had anxiety symptoms. I have had migraines from the time I was three and through my childhood and adult life have had a very busy brain. I mentally counted things, and after I learned to type in seventh grade, I used to mentally type whole conversations as they took place. I was an extremely fast typist.

The older I got, the worse the anxiety got, and the worse it got, the more I sucked it up and the harder I tried. I pedaled faster and slept worse. I couldn't understand it. I had a great job, a loving husband, and children I adored. I was a room parent at the girls' school, auction cochair, and reliable contributor for every occasion requiring cookies. But I was so twitchy I could barely make it through a single episode of *My Little Pony.*

In my worldview, this nameless dread was a character flaw.

It took a wild ride on the menopause Tilt-A-Whirl to propel my sorry self into the office of psychiatrist Judith Nowak. The nervous energy and hyperactivity that had once just been a nuisance were now making me plain crazy. A witch's brew of brain and sex hormones combined to give me insomnia, auditory hallucinations, and free-floating anxiety so intense that coffee slopped out of the mug held in my trembling hand. I was in a state of free-floating, gut-wrenching, nameless terror most of the time. My brain boiled with noise and music, and not in a good way. I was as likely to hear shrieking repetitions of "Bingo Was His Name-O" as one of Bach's Brandenburg Concertos.

Dr. Nowak called the noise in my brain *auditory hallucinations* and diagnosed it as a form of obsessive-compulsive disorder. I started taking antianxiety medication, but it took us months to get the cocktail right. In the meantime, when the noise was especially loud, I would calm myself by having pretend, mental conversations with Sharon. I would imagine asking her a question or telling her a joke, and I would mentally answer back as I thought she would.

One day I was having a mental conversation with Sharon about my daughters. I was doing my human best, but the kids needed more of everything than I had. Little Josie at age five was utterly charming, but she'd throw furious tantrums now and then. When I tried to plus-up my love and attention, she repulsed me like I was a green vegetable. Meantime her older sister, Grace, stored up a mother lode of grievance at my supposed preference for her screeching sibling. Whining and raging rang throughout the family home.

I am a highly conflict-averse person. I don't get angry, I don't fight, and I don't yell. My rational response to conflict between the girls was to do what I *always* do when somebody's pissed: get out of the way. And then their behavior really went south, as they tried to capture my attention, while I retreated because I wasn't making them happy. I didn't get it until John took me aside gently and said, "Burk, you can't withdraw emotionally from the kids. They can't stand it."

Well, that certainly stung, coming from a man who doesn't exactly wear his heart on his sleeve. But John was right. He understood our children better than I did. And he understood that I just couldn't come up with the chops to move toward them when they were furious and obnoxious—that is, when they needed me most.

As I was mulling this, with music shrieking in my brain, I found myself actually praying. I eliminated the middlewoman, Sharon, and was having a mental conversation with God. I mentally said what I would have said to her: *This is really hard. The brain noise and insomnia and shakiness and fear are really kicking my butt. Help. Please help me be a good mother.*

That was it. Just "Help." I believe I plagiarized my very first prayer. Anne Lamott wrote, "Here are the two best prayers I know: 'Help me, help me, help me,' and 'Thank you, thank you, thank you.'" I didn't know I believed in God, and I didn't know to whom I was praying, but "Help me" was the only prayer I had in me.

And here is the miracle. Help came. The prayer went in and out of my head and I forgot about it. But a heavy weight floated off my heart, and from one moment to the next, motherhood seemed doable again. When I entered my front door, two little girls mobbed me for hugs, and the world was a warm and welcoming place. Aww...

But let's not get ahead of ourselves. Since I was not a believer, I assumed the answered "help me" prayer was a fluke. I didn't pray again for months. Then, one Saturday afternoon while walking home from Capitol Hill's Eastern Market, I saw three big, tall, teenage dudes with jeans sliding down their hips approaching from the opposite direction. My brain clenched in an involuntary spasm of middle-aged white woman fear and loathing of all things hip-hop. It was broad daylight and these guys weren't even looking at me, but there I was, channeling George Wallace. I silently breathed the second prayer of my life: *God, please help me not to be a racist butthead.*

There is so much about God and faith and the Bible and Christians I don't understand. But there is this one true thing that I do know that keeps me reading and seeking and following and believing. I asked for help when I knew my own supply of kindness and confidence wasn't enough to get me across six feet of sidewalk. And God answered my prayer.

A load of ugliness and fear and anxiety vanished. I walked by the low-pants guys. They walked by me. I didn't feel like a racist. I felt great. The Lord went back to his list of wonders to perform.

six

Whirling
Dervish-ness

don't know why I have whirling dervish disorder. I wish I knew. Maybe it means I am searching for God. Nah, it's craziness, plain and simple. But there *is* a theory about whirling dervish-ness and God that I find quite fascinating.

A Catholic theologian named Ronald Rolheiser has written an extraordinary book called *The Holy Longing* about how we are hard-wired to long for something beyond ourselves. He grabbed me immediately, writing about restlessness, longing, and the search for God. "All life is fired by longing. The simplest of plants and the highest of human love have this in common—yearning, restlessness, a certain insatiable pressure to eat, to grow, to breed, to push beyond self." Rolheiser called this life force the "fire of God."

I don't know about the pressure to breed, but insatiable pressure to eat is something I can relate to. And so is that yearning and restlessness after something more beautiful and bigger and greater than I can hold in my two hands. The music I love stirs up that yearning and sadness and fierce desire to possess. I grew up with classical music, and I associate it still with everything good. As a nonbeliever, the beauty of a Brahms symphony would sear my heart. I couldn't hold on to that beauty; I couldn't create it myself, though I tried as a classical pianist for many years.

When I was in my teens, I fell in love with the greatest of all sopranos, Leontyne Price. I had a turntable, and our Ames, Iowa, library had dozens of albums of Leontyne Price singing opera, gospel, and German lieder. I checked them out and listened to my goddess sing Tosca, Aida, and Bess. Best of all was "Ride On, King Jesus," a spiritual so gorgeous it nearly killed me. Really. I could not bear the beauty. I would listen to that particular recording over and over just to be able to take the edge off the pain of absolute, searing, eviscerating beauty. I think this is what Rolheiser meant by holy longing.

I met Leontyne Price in 1971 when she did a sold-out recital in my hometown of Ames. She sang the arias and art songs and spirituals that I'd memorized from her recordings. There she was, in the flesh—my idol. She had a gigantic Afro, enormous pearls, and that extraordinary voice. And she was statuesque and commanding. She killed us all. She brought down the house in wave after wave of standing ovations. We couldn't bear to let her leave the stage.

Stunningly, she not only left the stage but came to my house. My father was then the head of the music department at Iowa State University. In those days, Ames didn't have a restaurant that served meals after 10:00 p.m. Leontyne Price, like most singers, did not eat before her performance. When it was over, she was hungry. We drove her home with the finest accompanist of all time, Dalton Baldwin, and had ham sandwiches and beer in our living room. She was as beautiful up close as she was onstage, and she was kind to all of us. I shyly told her that I worshiped her singing and that her title role in *Porgy and Bess* was my favorite.

But hearing her sing live and meeting her in person didn't actually lessen that indescribable sorrow and yearning to capture and hold beauty. It was a holy longing—that comingled grief and joy and outrage, for want of a better word, at ravishing beauty. We're hard-wired for something bigger and greater and more beautiful than ourselves. We worship Olympic athletes (well, maybe you do—I worship operatic sopranos) for their perfection, but it is never enough, is it?

I've come to think that we're supposed to yearn for the unattainable. It is a compulsion to go off the grid, pushing us beyond what we know into unfamiliar territory. I spent virtually my entire adult life yearning for something that I most assuredly could not conjure up myself. Goodness knows, I tried. I studied classical piano for twenty-five years and wanted it to be beautiful. I wanted to sing like Price and to look like her too. I wallowed in Brahms, Chopin, Rachmaninoff and soaked in opera, choral music, chamber quartets, and symphonies. And on a more prosaic note, I was so consumed with anxiety and longing that I tried to outrun it by staying busy. Insanely busy. I baked, sewed, jogged, volunteered, sang, worked full time, and did Christmas, Easter, and Thanksgiving with both hands.

Blaise Pascal, a seventeenth-century mathematician and philosopher, had a perspective on this. Blaise, who was plenty manic himself, scrawled his random thoughts in tiny script all over his notebooks—in the margins, upside down, around in circles, and the like. Some of the notations are bizarre and unexplained fragments like "You're killing me," "prison cell," and "Cleopatra's nose." But on some pages of his famous *Pensées* you find the most profound thoughts about existential angst that have ever been written.

Like this: "What does this [human] greed and helplessness proclaim, except that there was once within us true happiness of which all that now remains is the outline and empty trace? Man tries unsuccessfully to fill this void with everything that surrounds him, seeing in absent things the help he cannot find in those that are present, but all are incapable of it."

Got that right. I never succeeded in keeping my demons at bay by dancing as fast as I could, but it didn't stop me from trying. Here in the Middle Kingdom, we lurk halfway between God and animals, knowing we'll die and be tormented by beauty and goodness that are beyond our grasp. It's painful, and we sure do know it. It is not for nothing that people throughout all ages and from every walk of life get blind drunk, hurt each other, work to oblivion, screw their brains out, and crochet too many potholders.

I think we search our whole lives for what can fill that God-shaped emptiness. Yet out of that yearning and striving comes the Internet, the Mars rover, the Brahms *Alto Rhapsody*, Olympic gymnasts, and the Washington National Cathedral. The most creative and innovative people have ants in their pants. They are uncomfortable with the limits of skin, mind, and gravity, and they yearn to conquer it.

Sometimes it drives them crazy. Or their craziness makes them creative. Mental illness, particularly bipolar disorder, is closely linked with creativity. Kay Redfield Jamison, a professor of psychiatry and herself a person with bipolar disorder, is the author of a stunning book on the connection between creativity and bipolar disorder.

In *Touched with Fire: Manic-Depressive Illness and the Artistic Temperament,* Jamison wrote that modern psychiatry does not cure acute psychosis, although treatment for people with depression and bipolar disorder, in particular, can provide considerable relief to some. But with or without treatment, individuals with debilitating mental illness have made a breathtaking contribution to poetry, music, and art.

Dr. Jamison counted eighty-three major poets with probable manic-depressive illness or major depression, including the greatest creative minds the Western world has ever known: John Keats, William Blake, Robert Burns, Emily Dickinson, Lord Byron, Samuel Taylor Coleridge, William Cowper, T. S. Eliot, Edna St. Vincent Millay, Boris Pasternak, Sylvia Plath, Edgar Allan Poe, Ezra Pound, Alexander Pushkin, Percy Bysshe Shelly, Alfred Lord Tennyson, Dylan Thomas, and Walt Whitman.

Thirty of the poets on the Jamison list were institutionalized. Thirty-two attempted suicide. Twenty of them succeeded. It is the same in the field of classical music. Robert Schumann suffered the agony of mania and depression—classic bipolar disorder, based on the symptoms he described—and created works of such surpassing beauty that one can scarcely hear them without bursting into tears. Tchaikovsky, Handel, Mozart, Rachmaninoff, Mahler, and many other composer's also appear to have had mental illnesses involving profound mood swings.

Could it be that their music and poetry were a lifesaving outlet for them, buying them years or decades more than they otherwise would have had? Or is it that that these composers and poets were so tortured by the beauty they carried in their brains and hearts that they could not live easily, or very long, in this world? God knows.

I have an artist friend, Marlene, whose favorite words of the Bible are the first five: "In the beginning God created." If we are indeed made in his-or-her image, then we are meant to create as well. Maybe we're all a bit uncomfortable in our own skin because God made it a bit too big on purpose so we'll stretch and reach and grow to fit the pattern we were cut from.

One of my girls' favorite books when they were very small was *Miss Rumphius.* I read it aloud so many times I can remember whole pages. Miss Rumphius was told as a little girl that she must do something to make the world a more beautiful place. She had many aspirations in life and grew up to achieve them all—travel the world, build a house by the sea. But she still hadn't made the world a more beautiful place. One day she hit upon the notion of planting lupine flower seeds everywhere, and she did that until the end of her life, scattering them all over creation.

I don't think that using our overabundance of energy and talent—the fire of God—for the purpose of entertaining or comforting ourselves will fill our God-shaped yearning. We have to stretch and reach for something braver and grander and finer than we are, not to make ourselves grander and finer, but so we can help make our world fit the pattern it was cut from. That is to say, full of music and kindness and lupines.

We can either scratch our mysterious itch, like the evil-tempered rhinoceros in Kipling's *Just So Stories,* until it wrinkles and folds and we're still pissed off. Or we can grow into it by raising our eyes from our irritating, prickly, ants-in-the-pants selves and looking for something to do or create that makes the world a more beautiful place while we treasure its creatures.

Nine years ago God gave me a dog for my fiftieth birthday. Well, actually it was my husband who gave me the dog, but my dog Fala is so entwined with my coming to believe in God that I like to give him-or-her the credit.

The family needed a pet. John irrationally dislikes cats (I love them), and I was equally intransigent on the issue of birds, rodents, reptiles, and fish. The girls voted for a Pomeranian; I wanted a German shepherd. We compromised on a German shepherd.

From the day she arrived as a nine-week-old purebred puppy, Fala was completely devoted to me and the family. She followed me around the house wherever I went and lay across my feet when I paused. Nobody in my life has ever been so glad to see me when I come home.

But Fala had other classic shepherd traits that were quickly apparent: she was extremely protective of me and the kids and implacably hostile to strangers. I trained and socialized her as best I could, but as she grew to a gorgeous eighty-five pounds, the number of my friends willing to act as training bait dwindled. She would charge and bark furiously at anybody crossing our threshold. When I took her to the girls' soccer game, she ran out onto the field and tried to drag Josie out of the game.

I took Fala to two different training schools on the advice of dog pros around the neighborhood. In both cases she was physically abused by idiot trainers, which exacerbated her fear aggression considerably. I took her for an assessment by a behavioral veterinarian who—from a distance of about ten feet—told me that I should give her up.

I didn't. Because of Fala's connection to me, it would have broken both our hearts for her to be farmed out to strangers. Euthanasia would be kinder. So I kept her and worked very hard over the next eight years to keep everybody safe.

Fala's job, in her mind, was to protect me from mass murderers—that is to say, my friends, neighbors, relatives, and people walking down the street. When she was about a year old, I started training her with a Frisbee, and she got very good at catching it. That dog wanted to work, and having a Frisbee-catching job kept her from doing her other job.

Fala taught me more than how to toss a Frisbee. She taught me about love—hers for me, mine for her. Bishop Kevin was right: dogs love us unconditionally. They don't care if we're a success or failure; in their eyes, we are perfect, and they adore us. And I adored her, no matter how difficult she was. She didn't have to earn it or deserve it or understand it. I just loved her.

Fala also taught me about fear. I came to understand that she would try to attack anything she was afraid of. "Fear biters" is what my vet called dogs like Fala. It is not for nothing that German shepherds are used for protection. When frightened, they will go after the scary thing, as opposed to the golden retriever approach, which is to lie on their back with four feet sticking up and smile.

I came to learn, slowly, about my own fear from being with Fala. I didn't know it at the time, but I must have gotten a German shepherd so I'd look tough. In reality, I'm very timid. For one thing, I'm a small woman, which means I've got that ever-present sense that at any moment somebody might enjoy mugging me. But I'm also just basically a coward. I hated being alone. I almost never walked around the neighborhood, and I locked the house obsessively. If I came home in the evening and the house was empty, I'd check under all the beds and in the closets.

Fala changed all that. She taught me to love the outdoors—we walked together every single day to all the neighborhood parks. And I felt completely safe in my little house, day or night. As a matter of fact, most days we didn't even lock the front door. There is no way on earth that anybody could get in without Fala knowing it and shredding them.

My friend Laurie told me that dogs can be marvelous service animals for adults and children with emotional or developmental disabilities. I made some crack about a Chihuahua running to the rescue with a tiny bottle of Valium around its neck. But seriously, it's a wonderful, majestic thing, what dogs can do. Laurie told me that after she had been sexually assaulted, she was frightened all the time. Then she got a gigantic black Doberman pinscher named Soma. She never had to be afraid again.

My dog was so attuned to me that I had to watch what I said around her. I was excitedly telling John about some outrageous thing in the newspaper one morning, when he said quietly, "Burk, look at your dog." Fala was sitting bolt upright and staring at me alertly, pupils dilated hugely, and ready to leap into action. "Mom's excited! Who do I bite?" I came to realize that I had to be very calm and very strong when I was with her or she would do her Protection Job. When I was calm, she was calm. As Sharon put it, "God gave you Fala to make you calm and brave. You can't both be hysterical."

Sharon herself was the only stranger my dog liked. Sharon earned it: she visited the house every day for a month after first meeting Fala, first tossing and then handing over cheese cubes.

Fala loved cheese cubes. One time Sharon came over to the house, knocked, and got no answer. The front door was unlocked, so she came on in. Fala was upstairs with me, and I heard her go roaring down the stairs. She tore up to Sharon, then came to a screeching halt, inches away. Some dim memory clicked on in her lemon-sized brain. "Cheese-cube lady!" She put her paws on Sharon's shoulder and licked her face. Sharon told me later, "Gosh, I'd hate to have been off by one dog treat."

It seems cosmically right that Fala and Sharon loved each other. I don't actually know the moment I came to believe—it was such a quiet, cautious, lengthy process that it's impossible to pinpoint the transition from unbeliever to Christian—but Fala and Sharon were all wrapped up in it. We three walked together all over Capitol Hill. Sharon and I talked about faith, and Fala growled at strangers. Sharon, my friend and spiritual mentor, and Fala, my frightened dog who loved me unconditionally, were God's sweetest gifts during those years of confusion and seeking and questioning.

That's my conversion story, and I'm sticking to it.

Fala died of throat cancer last spring. Her illness and death completely gutted me. I missed her so much. I was so used to having a big dog at my side I didn't know what to do with my hands. I kept reaching down to stroke her and she wasn't there. My bad girl was gone; I felt like I'd lost a couple of limbs. I cried for weeks—at work, at home, at meetings, with friends, with perfect strangers. The solution seemed obvious: Fala just needed to come back, and everything would be fine.

I wanted to get another dog, and I promised John it would be young and not a German shepherd. Having lost Fala at the age of eight, I sure wasn't prepared to go through that again anytime soon. But I learned through a friend about a German shepherd breeder in Tulsa, Oklahoma—a convenient fifteen hundred miles away from Washington, DC—with a four-year-old German shepherd. Banshee was a black, long-coat, former show dog with hip dysplasia. She could still run and walk without limping, but she wasn't breeding stock. She needed a home. I needed her.

I drove to Tulsa with my friend Sandy Gavin. We met Banshee, who was named inappropriately. When they brought her out to meet me, she licked me on the cheek, then lay down happily. When it was time to leave, she hopped into Sandy's car and never looked back.

Banshee, who looks terrifyingly like an enormous black wolf, is now called Bonnie. Like Fala, she loves me to death. But unlike Fala, she doesn't bark at all, much less go into an Abu Ghraib routine every time somebody walks by the house: when strangers come to the door, Bonnie grins at them.

I am so grateful for this dog. I am so grateful for the daily, visible evidence of a God who loves me exactly as I am and gave me just what I needed. Right now, that visible sign is curled up by my side, perfectly happy. And so am I.

seven

A Leap of Faith

joined IJM in 2006, less than a year after believing in God. I admit the timing is somewhat suspect. I desperately wanted to work for IJM, but IJM wouldn't hire me because I wasn't a Christian. I became a Christian, and they hired me.

Don't you judge! There's more to the story!

My excruciatingly awkward journey to joining IJM began in 2003. I had become wholly disillusioned with my work as a human rights advocate, and I was increasingly attracted to IJM's service to victims of violence. The way the organization worked—right in the trenches—was a radical departure from the advocacy and lobbying I'd done throughout my career at Human Rights Watch and Physicians for Human Rights. Still a very young organization, IJM was scarcely known in the conventional human rights field. Moreover, virtually everybody I knew professionally was skeptical at best and contemptuous at worst about IJM's Christian identity.

I thought long and hard about leaving the established human rights field, where I had made something of a name for myself, for an upstart Christian organization trying to do something no one else had imagined possible. It didn't matter; I wanted in. I had been involved in policy and advocacy for decades, and I was tired of writing and speaking about human rights violations. I wanted to help an organization that actually brought relief to violated and exploited people, one case at a time.

In my vanity, I thought that my pals Gary Haugen and Sharon Cohn would be thrilled to hire me. I wrote to Gary and pronounced my willingness to quit my job and come work for IJM. To my amazement, Gary stalled for time by not answering my lavishly self-promoting e-mail. I wrote another. Ringing silence.

I didn't get the job. I didn't know that IJM wouldn't hire me because I was not a Christian. Call me dumb (you may), but it absolutely did not occur to me that this all-Christian organization would turn me away. I was their friend and IJM's biggest champion. But I'd given my beloved friends Gary and Sharon a problem. Remember, Gary and Sharon were my spiritual mentors. They knew I wasn't a believer because we talked about it constantly. They knew I was teetering on the edge of faith, and they knew I would be wounded and almost certainly alienated from them and from God if they rejected me as a colleague.

I was desperately hurt and quite ready to chuck an eight-year friendship over Gary's silence. Sharon, bless her, told me to simply talk to Gary. So we talked. Gary told me that the timing for hiring me was not right. The organization wasn't quite ready to create a position for a government relations expert, as I wanted to be for IJM. But he also said that IJM was a Christian organization, and I wasn't in a place, spiritually, to thrive there. He knew full well that I believed in Sharon and I believed in him, but I didn't believe in God.

I don't know why I didn't simply walk away from Gary, Sharon, and IJM and never look back. Then and now I detested exclusivity, and I don't take rejection lightly. But somehow, Gary found the words to honor our friendship and my desire to work with him. And God must have given me ears to hear them even though I didn't know it at the time.

Our friendship rebounded the minute we talked. As he crossed the room to join me in a coffee shop, I shouted, "Where the hell have you been?" He laughed, we hugged, and somehow it was fine. I stayed on at my job at Physicians for Human Rights, working with people I loved on an issue I cared passionately about: the global HIV/AIDS pandemic.

For the next three years I got to work side by side with HIV-treatment activists who were literally reinventing the public health field. It was an honor. Seeing what the US government could do when Republicans and Democrats worked together on global AIDS healed some of the despair I felt after the Rwanda genocide, when official Washington did absolutely nothing. Looking back at what I learned in those years, I'm so thankful that Gary and Sharon didn't hire me in 2003. It wasn't the right time yet.

Three years later, out of the blue, Gary's assistant called, asking me to come by to meet with Gary and his chief operating officer. We talked for hours about what IJM needed to "scale up and replicate" poor people's access to justice, the way the United States had scaled up Africa's access to antiretroviral drugs. I hardly realized it, but we were talking about IJM creating a new position, vice president for government relations. They invited me to apply.

Part of the application process at IJM requires candidates to submit a statement of faith. Mine was rather feeble, but it was the truest thing I have written before or since. In it, I described my un-faith journey and how, over the past years, I'd come to finally find the good God I hadn't believed existed. It went something along these lines: "I'm a disaster, but I prayed for help and I got it. When I pray, I'm less of a disaster. For this I have a grateful heart." The interview process was kindly, and faith issues weren't a problem until the very last person I talked to.

It was Ken Germer, vice president of human resources at the time. He was one of IJM's first employees in their very early days, and I had met him through Gary and Sharon long before joining IJM. Ken is a very funny man—we usually bust out laughing the minute we see each other. But at my hiring interview, my hilarious friend was dead serious. After assuring me that I'd passed my interviews with flying colors, Ken asked me to consider whether I really wanted to join a Christian organization like IJM.

He told me that people at IJM actually believe that God is responsible for rescuing our clients and putting rapists and pimps and slave owners in jail. Ken also reminded me of the enormous resources IJM invests in prayer, including quarterly spiritual retreats and a yearly gathering where hundreds of people come to Washington for three days to do nothing but pray for IJM's staff and clients.

As Ken put it, "If you aren't a believer, it is going to seem to you like a huge waste of time." He told me that IJM had hired people who had chafed because of the emphasis on faith and ended up leaving. He was too fond of me to see me chafe and scratch and eventually leave the organization we both loved.

"Fine, fine," I said. "No problem." I knew I was right for this job and it for me. Okay, I wasn't a pray-out-loud kind of person, but I'd been to 11:00 prayer. I had been visiting IJM for years, at Sharon's invitation, to give speeches about my human rights career to each semester's new class of interns. I started sticking around for 11:00 prayer. Nothing weird happened. No glossolalia, no swaying with arms above the head. Just lovely, quiet, Quaker-meeting-style prayer about things that mattered. Larry Martin, an IJM staff person I didn't know, had even prayed for me, which touched me deeply.

Then Ken dropped his bombshell. "Have you heard about 8:30 stillness?" No, I had not. Turns out that the IJM workday starts at 8:30. The front doors are locked, and phones and computers are silenced. IJM'ers sit at their desks and pray for thirty minutes. Every single day.

It was a deal breaker. I have obsessive-compulsive disorder and clinical anxiety. I can't sit still for thirty seconds, much less thirty minutes. Moreover, I hated the concept of an enforced spiritual discipline. My anarchist hackles rose. Ken was probably right. The commitment to prayer was going to make me crazy. Crazier. The next day I called him and withdrew my application.

Ken was in a panic. He really wanted me to join IJM, but

he wanted me to be happy there. IJM's chief operating officer at the time, Bob Lonac, called me, and he couldn't have been kinder. "Holly? You're going to be fine at IJM. The faith stuff is going to be fine." Bob knew I was a baby believer with a chip on my shoulder—but he also knew, as new as my faith was, it was true. He made a gigantic leap of faith in offering me the job, and I made a leap of faith to trust him. My cooler head prevailed. I accepted the job. And even though I'm very different than most of the staff in my spiritual disciplines, I can sometimes sit quietly for three of the thirty minutes. The rest of the time I write. But Ken was correct when he described how much time and resources IJM devotes to God. I have come to value it, and I participate in it.

Now I have to defend it. In early January 2009, the *New Yorker* published a lengthy profile on Gary Haugen. The writer, Samantha Power, knows and loves IJM. She'd traveled with Gary and other staff to see our work in Asia and Africa and came back really jazzed about it. Her article was overwhelmingly positive, except for one thing. Our Christian identity took one hell of a beating.

Aryeh Neier, a leading figure in the human rights field, was quoted in the article: "If it is objectionable to limit employment by reasons of race, I think it is comparably objectionable to limit by reason of religion." I know Aryeh very well. He founded Human Rights Watch, where I worked for fourteen years. He was my mentor, friend, and boss for ten of them. I admire him and I owe him. Unhappily, Aryeh is so repulsed by IJM's Christian identity that we've had almost no communication since I came here.

Aryeh comes by his views about discrimination honestly. His family survived the Holocaust, and he spent five years as a child in a displaced persons camp in England. He has devoted his life to freedom of speech and thought, and he believes to the very core of his being that discrimination of any kind, for any reason is a slippery slope right into a toxic waste dump of abuses and injustice.

In 1977, when Aryeh was national director of the American Civil Liberties Union, the group sued the overwhelmingly Jewish city of Skokie, Illinois, for prohibiting American Nazis from marching through the community. Aryeh Neier demanded freedom for white supremacists, skinheads, and Nazi wannabes to speak and march, knowing that it would be the best antidote for the poison they spewed. He called it "defending my enemies."

Aryeh was right on Skokie, but I think he's wrong about IJM. Look at it this way. Non-Christians would not be remotely interested in joining IJM if it were a Christians-only organization that translated Bibles or built churches or sent missionaries overseas. Aryeh and the ACLU have never sued the Wycliffe Bible Translators for refusing to hire non-Christians. It is simply a given that Christians have the right to restrict their group's membership to fellow Christians if they engage in religious activities. It would be decidedly bizarre if atheists, Muslims, or Jews wanted to join them.

Now let's look at religious groups that engage in nonreligious activities, like the Catholic orders working in mission hospitals or schools. I think it's a safe bet that civil libertarians are not beating down the doors to these all-Christian organizations. Why not? Why can't non-Christians join the Maryknoll Sisters and teach kindergarten in Guatemala? There have been no lawsuits to answer the question, perhaps because prayer, celibacy, and poverty come with the Maryknoll package.

Now consider IJM. Gary Haugen created an organization not to distribute tracts or translate Scripture but to provide free legal services to the poor, and we impose no religious test on those we serve. There is nothing inherent to IJM's service to our clients that a nonbeliever couldn't also do. But IJM is like a missionary group or a religious order in that its very existence is predicated on the Bible's call for the people of God to serve victims of injustice.

Ken Germer was right. If you were not a Christian believer, the hundreds of hours at IJM spent in prayer for God's help to do the work would just seem like a colossal waste of time, not to mention extremely weird. Our uniform is even a version of a nun's habit—it's a ruthlessly earnest business suit. All we'd have to do is add a celibacy clause to our hiring requirements for accusations of discrimination to stop dead.

Seriously, none of those things captures what's most

important about the Christian community that IJM provides. Although this truth may not resonate with nonbelievers, it is simply this: people at IJM need God's help to do the work. Some of us need God's help just to get up in the morning and put our shoes on the right feet. Shared belief in God is both glue and oxygen for IJM'ers, and the organization wouldn't exist without it. Secular folks or people of other faiths can and are doing the work of justice in other organizations. There are more than enough victims to go around.

eight

In the Company
of a Late Bloomer

remember the time my daughter Grace met Tun Channareth (known to us as Reth— rhymes with "jet"), a Cambodian land mine survivor and hero of the mine ban movement. Reth came to the United States in 1999 to do a tour with Jody Williams, who won the 1997 Nobel Peace Prize for leading the International Campaign to Ban Landmines. I went with them when they visited my home state of Iowa. It was a few weeks before Iowa's historic early presidential caucuses, and the place was swarming with presidential aspirants and reporters. Reth and Jody were there to challenge the candidates to support the Mine Ban Treaty.

Afterward, Reth came back to Washington, DC, with me for meetings with policymakers. I could hardly wait to get home. It was the longest I'd been away from Josie and Grace, who were only two and four years old, and we'd missed each other terribly. John and the girls were there to meet me when I arrived at Reagan National Airport with Reth and Jody. I wanted to hug the girls until they squeaked, but Reth was right behind me. I only had time to blurt, "You're going to meet my friend Reth—be polite," before he came rolling off the Jetway.

Reth's appearance is breathtaking. He wears short shorts to give himself maximum mobility. His superbly muscled arms and torso swing him in and out of his wheelchair in seconds. You can see how this guy traveled to every corner of his heavily mined country on the back of his buddy's motorbike, gathering thousands of signatures on a petition to ban antipersonnel land mines. One of Reth's legs is amputated high on the thigh, the other just below the knee. Both stumps are clearly visible. But once your brain stops searching frantically for the missing parts and your eyes travel to his beautiful face, you meet a man—not a double amputee.

Josie hid behind John, but Grace stood her ground. When Reth rolled over to her and said, "Hi, I'm Reth," she stuck out her little paw and shook his hand. Reth's charisma and love for children won her over. Within moments they were deep in conversation about his wooden wheelchair that he'd built himself, using bicycle wheels and salvaged scrap.

The minute he rolled away to get his luggage, Gracie turned to me and asked the obvious. "What happened to his legs?" I explained that they had been blown away.

"Blown away." Kids in mine-saturated countries like Angola and Mozambique, Cambodia and Chechnya know exactly what that means. But to my little daughter, "blown away" is something that happens to dandelion puffs in a breeze or a balloon that escapes from your hand. She looked at me and said soberly, "Mommy, the wind could never do that."

And there you have a perfect illustration of the randomness of suffering. My Gracie at four was so protected from ugliness in the world that she had no knowledge of weapons that tear off limbs and no vocabulary for explosions. Her child counterparts in Somalia, on the other hand, are literally tied with ropes to trees so they don't walk or crawl beyond a safe four-yard perimeter into invisibly mine-saturated ground only steps away.

Coming to believe in God did not answer the question of randomness or the unpredictability of miracles or the dismay of unanswered prayer. It just tantalized me with the prospect that there might be answers. I want them.

The randomness of who gets to live and who has to die is so painful that mostly I'd prefer not to think about it at all. But I was confronted by the issue very directly when I did some policy work on global HIV/AIDS in the early 2000s, before I had come to believe in a good God.

The HIV/AIDS pandemic was enough to knock anybody off their spiritual pins. The simple fact of the matter was that by 1997, if you had AIDS and lived in the United States or Europe, you could most likely obtain treatment that prolonged quality and years of life. But if you were a poor African with AIDS, you would certainly die. Scientists had cracked the code on life-prolonging antiretroviral drugs, but they were almost entirely unavailable in the developing world. When I became engaged in the campaign to provide access to treatment to Africa, six million people were HIV positive and in immediate need of treatment they didn't have. Hundreds of thousands of those infected every year were newborn babies of HIV-positive mothers.

In a scientific breakthrough, researchers discovered they could disrupt the transmission of HIV from mother to child by administering a course of antiretroviral drugs to a pregnant woman just before the delivery and to the infant for a period of time after the birth.

A nongovernmental organization called the Elizabeth Glaser Pediatric AIDS Foundation put the science to work, initiating testing of pregnant women and treatment before birth for HIV-positive mothers and their babies thereafter. They called it PMTCT—prevention of mother-to-child trans- mission. Approximately two-thirds of the infants receiving the therapy seroconverted, that is, they became HIV negative.

The Glaser Foundation lobbied Congress for funding to scale up PMTCT programs in countries with HIV prevalence. In March 2002, North Carolina Senator Jesse Helms, the Senate's most famous conservative, announced that he would secure five hundred million dollars for PMTCT initiatives in Africa.

But there was something desperately wrong with the Helms approach. The drugs offered in PMTCT programs saved babies but not their mothers. To keep an HIV-positive mother alive required a lifetime of expensive antiretroviral medication, not just a few days' supply.

I had a chance to talk to a Glaser staff member about using mothers' bodies for drug transmission to their infants but denying the women the same medication that would keep them alive to raise their children. No doubt, five hundred mil- lion dollars to prevent transmission of HIV to thousands of babies was a good thing; surely it was better that an infant should live than die. But saving a child so she could watch her mother die within a few years was unbearable. Babies who lose their mothers experience a world of grief, and then they usually die themselves. Is that what we were funding?

A friend from the Glaser Foundation said, "Of *course* it is a moral contradiction to save babies while their mothers die. Everyone will recognize that it is unconscionable to create tens of thousands of orphans. A program of treatment for mothers will have to be funded."

The old Marxist slogan about "heightening the contradictions" floated through my head. That is exactly what the babies-only treatment program did. It heightened the contradiction of saving the infants of dying mothers and pushed activists and policymakers, conservatives and liberals, into a very uncomfortable moral crevice.

Out of that awkward and painful crevice came something beautiful and good. Within two years, Senator Helms's five hundred million dollars for infants morphed into a five-year, fifteen-billion-dollar treatment program for women, men, and children in poor countries. He had bitterly opposed funding to combat America's own AIDS pandemic among gay men, but in his last term in office, the senator said publicly that he would have to answer to his Maker about what he'd done on HIV/AIDS. He wanted to have something to offer.

Mother Teresa was once asked how she came to pick up

forty-two thousand dying men, women, and children out of the gutters and off the sidewalks of India's cities. She answered that first she picked up one. And then another. If she had not picked up the one, she would never have helped the forty-two thousand. That's what we had going for us in the HIV treatment access movement. You see, if you can't demonstrate that it's possible to save one baby and one mother, then there won't be a moral imperative to save any. But once you've seen that miracle of one baby saved from HIV, it becomes unconscionable not to strain every sinew to save them all.

That's how I thought about the pitiless randomness of who gets to live and who dies from HIV/AIDS. It was a touchpoint of my faith journey, actually. When I worked on policy for three decades, it was not only emotionally necessary for me to float above individual suffering by looking at the disembodied universe of want, it was actually quite easy. But thinking of those newly HIV-negative infants at the breasts of dying mothers ripped my heart.

Randomness continues to challenge my fragile connection to God even now. Maybe especially now. Working for IJM, I not only experience the randomness of suffering, I also experience the randomness of rescue and restoration.

Four years ago, IJM discovered a sixteen-year-old girl, Mala, in a brothel in a dusty South Asian town several hours outside of the nearest large city. The child was terrified. The brothel was a place of absolute horror. Mala, who had been trafficked there about a year earlier, would later testify how she was raped and tortured by the brothel owner, Nakul Bera, and beaten if she refused customers. When she became pregnant, Bera beat her abdomen to induce a miscarriage.

Mala was frantic to get out of the brothel, but IJM couldn't simply remove her. My colleagues are not a substitute for the police; they had to persuade local law enforcement to rescue Mala. The team organized an operation with police to get her, but there was a tip-off, and by the time they arrived at the brothel, it was empty. Again IJM found the child, and again they took the information to police and accompanied them to the brothel to rescue her. She was gone.

Over the next several months, IJM tried seven times to rescue Mala. Each time the effort was tipped off and the girls were gone. On the eighth attempt, police and IJM staff entered the brothel. Mala was gone, but three young women were there, sleeping in a locked room. Our team was overjoyed to find the girls, who they had not previously known were there, but distraught that Mala was gone for the eighth time. An Indian colleague who was on the raid and accompanied the girls to the police station pulled out a picture of Mala and told an officer, "Lots of people care about this girl. You need to find her." Shortly thereafter, the policeman returned to the station with Mala on the back of his motorcycle. She had been given a new sari, which in haste had been put on backward.

Today, Mala is healthy and successful. She has a job she loves and lives in dignity and safety. Nakul Bera, the powerful brothel owner who raped, tortured, and trafficked Mala and many other girls has been tried and sentenced to ten years at hard labor in jail, against all odds.

Mala's case is a miracle and a mystery. I believe that God was in it, but I'm troubled all the same. Mala was raped a dozen times a day for weeks after IJM identified her. Why? The three girls we stumbled across on the eighth attempt to find Mala would be in prostitution to this day if previous efforts to rescue Mala had been successful. Why? But most of all, why was precious Mala saved but hundreds of thousands of others just like her are never known? Why, why, why?

If the randomness of suffering and rescue is almost unbearable to me, it is worse for our investigators in the field. These men, who pose as customers, know the names of children in prostitution and slaves in rice mills. They've talked with them, learned their stories, let them play games on their cell phones, and bought them Cokes. They give police their pictures and their locations in hopes that they will be rescued. Sometimes it works. Sometimes it doesn't.

I talked to IJM's top investigator who planned and carried out Mala's rescue and asked him how he could bear the work.

He said that he and all the investigators and social workers, who get so close to our clients, believe—they absolutely must believe in order to do the work—that suffering and injustice are God's to solve, not ours. "If we thought it all depended on us, that God didn't have a plan to make it right for all the victims, we would go mad," he said.

We talked, this good man and I, about the loaves and the fish. Jesus could have worked the miracle, but he first asked his followers to bring him what they had. "Yes," I said, "but the disciples got to see the five thousand fed. They didn't have to eat while others starved." That's what sticks in my craw: we hand over our pathetically inadequate tuna sandwiches in the midst of the famine, and we *don't get to see the miracle.* We live in the terrible knowledge that what happened to the one we saved is happening to untold others even while we're having this conversation.

My investigator friend, whom I can't name, sat quietly for a while. Then he described how, in the case of each girl who he has identified but not yet rescued, he has to go through a mental process of gathering up everything he knows about her, visualize her face, and then deliver the whole case over to God. He said, "I have to feel like I literally lay her at the feet of Jesus. I have done everything I can, but it is his work. I have to remind myself of that on every case."

My friend is able to live and work with joy in this crucible of random suffering and random rescue, and he is only able to do that because he believes what he cannot see: that God has a plan to redeem brokenness, find lost girls, and wipe away every tear from their eyes. We get to see glimpses of it. The rest is a mystery. If I ever get to meet the Lord, I'll ask for an explanation.

Answered and unanswered prayer, disappointments, and miracles run like an erratic electrocardiogram through my years at International Justice Mission. I am constantly torn between believing in miracles and not believing in them.

My IJM colleagues don't share my confusion and doubt about answered prayer. Their rock-solid belief is that God will literally intervene in response to prayer on behalf of our clients, our fund-raising, our speeches, our staff, our computers, and our sick relatives. We regularly hear reports at 11:00 prayer about how God answered our prayers and "showed up" at an intervention to take slaves from a brick kiln or in a courtroom where a man is sentenced to prison for the rape of a little girl or boy.

I was not a Christian for most of my adult life precisely because I did not see evidence that God cared enough about the world to intervene to save the tortured and the maimed and the insane and the abused. One of the most important things that got me over the hurdle was observing IJM, whose employees themselves "show up" to help widows and children and prisoners. God works through the people who love and serve him, and he gives them strength and courage. That made sense to me. I see it every day.

Moreover, answered prayer is the reason I came to faith: I asked for help and I got it. I absolutely believe that God answered my prayer to be peaceful, joyful, and patient. This is a mystery, and I'm never going to figure it out, but it is the truest thing I know about God because it happens to me. My character has changed because of prayer, and it keeps changing. The more often I pray, the more grateful, generous, and kind I am. When I don't pray, I'm my old self.

But intercessory prayer for God's tangible, miraculous intervention on behalf of others is harder for me to understand. God shows up for others because we asked him to? If indeed it is in my or our power to move God to action, then mustn't the converse be true? Would our failure to pray result in God withdrawing from us and withholding help from those who desperately need it?

Watchman Nee, a Chinese Christian, wrote a radical book, *Let Us Pray*, which takes this very view. He described how prayer is nothing less than God's people participating in God's work. That work, completed in heaven, will only be done on earth when it is requested. Nee wrote:

If the people of God fail to show sympathy towards
Him by yielding their will to Him and expressing their
one mind with Him in prayer, He would rather stand
by and postpone His work. He refuses to work alone.

But this can't be true. It is rather horrible to believe that
God requires our prayer to "show up." *We* need prayer to show
up for the poor and the miserable and the lonely and the sick.
Prayer doesn't change God; it changes us. God works through
his people, and we ask for his help through prayer. On the
other hand, God worked a miracle, quieting my brain and
calming my heart, because I asked and not before. Just because
it happened in my head doesn't make it less of a miracle than
an actual, touchable, tangible, physical change that occurs because I prayed for it. My own experience of answered prayer
suggests that at least part of what Watchman Nee said is right:
God did not speak into my anxiety and fear until I asked.

When I don't understand something, I put the question to
Google. When I don't understand God, I put the question to
Sharon or BibleGateway.com. This time I put the word *doubt*
into BibleGateway and up pops *Thomas,* which is now his last
name because his first has become for all time *Doubting,* poor
darling. He is the one disciple who didn't meet Jesus with the
others after the resurrection. Like the rest of us, he has doubts
about what he can't see with his own eyes. He needs to see a

little miracle before he'll believe in the big one. "Unless I see the mark of the nails in his hands, and put my finger in the mark of the nails and my hand in his side, I will not believe."

And that's why Jesus let Thomas see the miracle—so he would believe. I've got to figure this out: God answers some prayers and carries us forward with miracles along the way so that we might believe in the greatest miracle of all—that he exists.

To explain this, I've tried to think of a secular analogy. I mentioned earlier that my first German shepherd, Fala, was very fearful and hostile to strangers even as a puppy. I'd tried several trainers and various approaches, from prong collars to raw hamburger treats, and I still couldn't trust her not to jump somebody whose hat or umbrella she didn't like. A friend of mine, who is a sane person, told me about having an animal telepath named Diane come talk to her wacky Rhodesian ridgeback, Lucy. I am a firm nonbeliever in this crap, but I was desperate. I'd spent thousands of dollars on trainers, and nothing worked. What was another two hundred bucks?

I banished John and the girls from the house while I waited for Diane. Two o'clock arrived, and a comfortably dressed, sweet-faced, middle-aged woman knocked at the front door. Fala, who would ordinarily charge a stranger, came bounding up to Diane, then promptly sat down and cocked her head in that universal doggy gesture for "Say wha'?" Diane said quietly, "She thinks I am a trainer. Fala had a bad experience with a trainer."

I'll say. I hadn't even mentioned it to Diane, but two different trainers had treated Fala brutally, and she was scared to death of them. Diane put the dog at ease, and within a minute all three of us sat down to talk. Diane asks, "What do you want to tell Fala?" I blurt out something about how much I wish she wouldn't scare people who come to the house. Diane soundlessly conveys something to Fala, who by this time is snoozing at her feet.

We talk about this and that, which involves me babbling and Diane and Fala sending mind messages. Diane tells me that Fala misses her mother and brothers and sisters. She knows that Holly loves her and likes it when they go to the park. The stream in the park smells good.

Though I was awed by Diane, none of her intuitions about Fala were particularly compelling. It's hardly going out on a limb to report that a one-year-old puppy misses her littermates and likes the park. Then I ask what Fala thinks of my husband, John. Diane sits quietly with Fala for a moment. They aren't even looking at each other. Then Diane says two words: "Dad sleeps." She waits a moment, then says, "Dad coughs."

The hair on my arms stood to attention. John, who had smoked for about forty-five years, had a cold that had turned into bronchitis and asthma. Those decades of cigarettes were working their magic, and he was very sick. He napped for hours every day and had brutal coughing spells. There is no way Diane could have known this. There was no smoke smell in the house, because John always smoked outside. Diane had never met John. For all she knew, he was a clean-living triathlete. But Fala knew that John coughed and slept a lot.

People have asked me whether I learned anything for my two hundred bucks. I did, but more about faith than about dog training. I learned this: Diane really does communicate with animals, but I wouldn't have believed it if her conversation had been limited to ordinary doggy things. What gave me absolute confidence in Diane was the throwaway line about John sleeping and coughing. It wasn't a helpful observation for training Fala, but it was a little miracle. It was indubitably true, and it confirmed for me that the rest of what Diane communicated from Fala was true as well.

I've swung back and forth between doubt and faith since I first experienced God as real. I want to have my belief in Jesus ratified by some tangible fact, the way my confidence in Diane was inspired by an actual demonstration that she could intuit information from Fala. That's what Thomas wanted, and he received it, albeit with a mild rebuke.

It's an odd thing, this faith journey. Asking God for help to be the way I was meant to be—a treasured child—has transformed the way I think of myself. It has calmed my anxiety, and it has made me a wiser, kinder, gentler friend, wife, mother, and colleague. Those gifts are enormous. So why is it so easy to forget them? Doubting Thomas knew and loved Jesus for years, but he didn't believe in him until he could touch him. Me too.

Maybe I need more miracles than most to believe in a good God. I still have doubts after seven years with International Justice Mission. But what I see happening here is so impossible that it's becoming positively irrational not to believe that God's hand is in it and with such frequency that coincidence is simply not a plausible explanation.

A couple years ago, IJM investigators and local police rescued a teen girl, Suhana, from a brothel. She had been trafficked there when she was thirteen and had been raped hourly for three years. She recovered in an aftercare home and was doing so well that her counselors decided Suhana could take a job outside the shelter. She began her new work but was soon betrayed by someone she thought was a friend and re-trafficked back into prostitution.

When they learned that Suhana was gone, IJM's investigators quickly located her false friend and discovered that she had been trafficked to a city a thousand miles away. IJM's investigators and social workers in that city started to search for her.

Now let's talk about finding Suhana. She had been trafficked to a metropolis of eighteen million people with an estimated five hundred thousand women and girls in its sex industry.

IJM found Suhana within four months as she was getting into a bicycle cab with a client. She was in forced prostitution one moment and in the arms of her IJM social worker, Smita, the next. She's free. Things like this happen all the time at IJM. Things that absolutely can't possibly happen *do* happen.

Sean Litton, who heads IJM's overseas operations, told me of one of his first cases in IJM's newly founded Manila office in 2001. Sean was visiting an aftercare home for sexually abused children when a lawyer came rushing in to say that a trial was taking place at that very moment of a man who had allegedly raped a little girl, Mariah, who was now living at the shelter. The shelter staff begged Sean to help with the case.

Sean grabbed the file, and he and the child and a social worker literally ran to the courtroom. He had only minutes to talk with the victim, a hyperactive six-year-old with a disability that made it impossible for her to focus or speak straightforwardly. As Sean tells it, his heart sank as he tried to talk to the child. With no DNA or witnesses, child sexual assault cases usually turn on the victim's statement. This little girl could scarcely put two words together. He had no time to win her trust or coach her; they had to go immediately into that courtroom.

So Sean prayed. He asked God to do what neither he nor the child could do. They entered the courtroom, and the judge called for her testimony. The defendant was right in the same courtroom, so Sean, kind man and fine lawyer that he is, placed himself between the child and her assailant. The judge came down off the bench and gently asked the child to describe what happened to her.

And then, the miracle: Mariah told of the assault in a clear, calm, and organized way, leaving out no detail and providing the information so persuasively that there wasn't a doubt in the room that she spoke the truth. The judge asked her, "Can you identify the man who hurt you?" Sean's little client stood up tall and brave, and craning her neck to see the man behind Sean, she said, "He's standing right there." Justice was done in the case.

My friend Joe Kibugu from Kenya rescued a young teenager who was so brutally raped that her hip was dislocated. She had a surgery that left her with a limp. Joe preached a sermon at a local church, and the head of Nairobi's best hospital happened to be in the congregation. Hearing about Joe's client, he immediately offered her free surgery and hospital care. The child and her damaged hip were wholly restored. Joe said, "I don't need to see Jesus turn water into wine. I wouldn't trust myself around all that wine anyway. This was miracle enough for me."

"Unless you see signs and wonders you will not believe."

Jesus knew us so well, Thomas and me and you. He knew we needed miracles to know him as miraculous. It has been that way for me. Finding Suhana and hundreds of other miracles that I've heard about with my own ears and seen with my own eyes are gifts from the Lord that I might believe. And when I believe, I might also believe what I do not see: that he has something more in mind than I can imagine for all those little ones who suffer.

Mother Teresa, an Albanian-born sister of Loretto, had been teaching at a school in India for a decade when she heard God insistently commanding her to serve the poorest of the poor. She referred to these visitations as "Voices." As she put it in a letter to her religious superior, she heard God saying, "There are plenty of nuns to look after the rich and well to do people—but for my very poor, there are absolutely none. For them I long—them I love. Wilt thou refuse?"

It was a miracle, and she heard God's miraculous voice many times more, always asking her to serve the poorest of the poor. Mother Teresa begged, bullied, and lobbied the Catholic hierarchy until the pope gave her permission to leave the Sisters of Loretto and begin her work as a Missionary of Charity in the slums of Calcutta. For the next fifty years, Mother Teresa attracted thousands of followers who lived and worked with the world's poorest people. Her homely face and blue-

and-white wimple became a beloved universal symbol of piety and charity. In 1979 she was awarded the Nobel Peace Prize.

When the Catholic Church published Mother Teresa's letters in 2007, it was in flagrant opposition to the nun's pleas that her private writings be destroyed. If you read them, you will understand her request. They are pitifully intimate revelations to her confessors of a heart and mind tormented by doubt, worthlessness, and alienation. The "Saint of Calcutta" suffered from profound spiritual darkness almost her entire adult life until her death in 1997.

It was the similarity of Mother Teresa's spiritual crisis to my grandmother's that persuaded me to set aside my revulsion for the church's violation of her privacy and read the letters. Perhaps in Grandmother Adah Wenger's Catholic counterpart I could find some insight into the mystery of deeply devout Christians who are abandoned by God.

What her spiritual confessors knew—and now we know as well—is that the moment the church granted her request, God's voice fell silent. It was not that Mother Teresa stopped believing in God. Rather, she could not feel his presence and felt despised and abandoned by him.

One of her letters describes an excruciating dissonance between her evangelistic message to dying street people and the aridity and loneliness of her own soul: "The place of God in my soul is blank. There is no God in me. When the pain of longing is so great—I just long and long for God, and then it is that I feel He does not want me. He is not there. I help souls—to go where?"

The executor of Mother Teresa's beatitude, Father Brian Kolodiejchuk, obviously believed that bringing the letters to light would contribute to the campaign for her sainthood. He stated that the letters reveal aspects of Mother Teresa's spiritual life, including "her intimate sharing in the Cross of Christ during her long years of interior darkness."

To this ordinary mortal, however, the letters are desperately sad and very troubling. Mother Teresa's personal experience of God is of one who takes pleasure in depriving her of virtually everything, including, most especially, himself: "Heaven from every side is closed.... If this brings You glory, if You get a drop of joy from this…if my suffering satiates Your Thirst,…here I am, Lord."

In terms of evangelism, that is very tough to sell. Who can possibly be attracted to a God who endlessly tortures a four-foot-tall nun who, at his command, gave up every material comfort to live among the destitute and dying? Mother Teresa's Jesus appears to be cruelly withholding—and utterly deaf to her desperate cries.

Frederick Buechner wrote that faith is a lifelong search for the source of all goodness and truth that we glimpse briefly and joyously only to lose and find and lose again. Such was the case with my grandmother Adah, whose weeks- or months-long periods of darkness were always followed by a return to mental health. And her faith returned with it, full of intelligence, serenity, and gratitude.

But we don't have that comfort from Mother Teresa's story. Having palpably experienced God's presence in her childhood and young adulthood, the connection was severed when she was thirty-eight years old, and it was never reattached. Over the decades she wrote continuously of her worthlessness and God's rejection of her. "How long will our Lord stay away?... The more I want him the less I am wanted.... He [God] is destroying everything in me.... The child of your love—and now become as the most hated one—the one You have thrown away as unwanted—unloved."

If Mother Teresa were not a world-famous, Nobel Prize–winning saint-in-the-making, one wouldn't feel compelled to make sense of this. But she was, and the publication of her private letters pushes her lifelong misery from God's absence right in our faces.

We have a couple of choices. We can decide that God was actually right at Mother Teresa's side, but because of mental illness she did not know it. That option would relieve us of the repulsive vision of God leaning down to abuse a devoted servant, but it leaves us, unacceptably, with a Creator who is available only to the mentally fit. Alternatively, we can choose to believe that Mother Teresa was not mentally ill and that God really was absent, presumably for some specific, albeit mysterious, purpose.

After two readings of her letters, I had no answer and was bone tired of both Mother Teresa and her God. Then I saw this sentence from her Nobel Prize acceptance speech that might be a key to something important about her work and faith: "Tuberculosis and cancer [are] not the real diseases. I think a much greater disease is to be unwanted, unloved."

Mother Teresa's mission was to provide healing and comfort for the "real diseases" of loneliness and estrangement. She did not see herself or the Missionaries of Charity as healthcare providers or social workers, and she warned the sisters repeatedly against assuming such roles. They did not provide modern medical care to thousands of dying people they picked up from the streets and brought to their hospices.

Critics of Mother Teresa have accused her sisters of washing patients with cold water and not providing as much as an aspirin for their pain. Whatever one might think of this austere approach to physical comfort for the poor they served, Mother Teresa imposed it upon herself and her nuns at least as stringently. Missionary sisters' only personal possessions are two cotton saris and a wooden bucket to wash them in.

There is a scene in Richard Attenborough's documentary film where Mother Teresa is inspecting a new home donated to the Missionaries of Charity in the Bronx, where the sisters will minister to destitute elderly women in dangerous neighborhoods. She moves through the building, shaking her head and clucking in distress over its modest comforts. The next scene shows Missionaries of Charity sisters tearing up carpets, dismantling drapes, and hauling bed frames and a piano outdoors to the trash.

Mother Teresa took this ironclad vow of poverty because of her conviction that people who own things do not want to give them away. Her Missionaries of Charity sisters had nothing to withhold and only love and kindness to give.

Let's apply her logic—that people give the most to the poorest when they themselves own the least—to Mother Teresa's spiritual possessions. Ordinary logic holds that those who best know God's love have the most to share. But for Mother Teresa, the reverse appears to be true: she gave away what she did not possess. The God who rejected her was her daily and hourly gift to those she believed he loved most passionately: the dying, the maimed, and the unwanted.

With her logic of poverty in mind, I find myself wondering, *If Mother Teresa had known intimacy with God, might she have hoarded it, as most of us do with our material possessions? If an intimate, personal relationship with God had been available to her, would the Lord's "little spouse," as she called herself, have been so tireless in securing it for others?*

Mother Teresa was a relentlessly driven person who desperately wanted to bring Jesus to the wretched of the earth. This compulsion, which I imagine in part stemmed from her own yearning to be loved, drove this tiny, mysterious woman to do unimaginably great things. But her identification with the unloved was a blessing and a curse. She made the under-world of the poorest a better place, as her Sisters of Charity do to this day. But she was pitifully driven, as well, from her own sense of worthlessness.

Mother Teresa's and Adah Wenger's estrangement from God is and always will be a mystery to me. But this I believe: when she was denied the joy of a personal, intimate relation-ship with the God she adored, Mother Teresa roamed the world, looking for the filthiest, loneliest scraps of humanity she could find. She touched and kissed and caressed them, carry-ing them in her arms and looking deeply and lovingly into their eyes. Feeling abandoned and unloved herself, she could not bear others to suffer the same.

And I know this too. Mother Teresa has forever trans-formed how we think about the despised and the abandoned and the deranged. The right to live and die in dignity as a treasured child of a loving God is their birthright, as it is ours. It is Mother Teresa's too. I hope that now, at last, she knows it.

nine

What Providence Means

To be honest, I didn't actually understand that it was our birthright to be loved until I became a mother. When Gracie and Josie were young, I read somewhere that children behave badly because they feel bad. It was often true with my girls. Sometimes my toddlers would screech, balk, sulk, and kick their heels on the floor simply because it was nap time. More often, though, it was because they needed me to notice them, love them, listen to them.

Time-outs are the punishment of choice for modern parents, but John and I never got into it. They sure beat the spankings and shamings of our own youth, but for our girls, sending them away was the worst thing we could do to them. Maybe they had separation anxiety from their early months in orphanages. Or maybe I'm the one who has it. But we tried once or twice to plunk the girls down by themselves when they were being obnoxious, and it made them crazy. Plan B was to sit together on the stairs and talk a little. I would hug them very hard and remind them that they were beloved. Then we'd go find a snack.

Unconditional love is every child's inalienable birthright. My therapist, Dr. Betty Ann Ottinger, talks about the "gleam in a parent's eye" for her child. She means the authentic expression of delight every time your child sees your face. I never thought I'd have that gleam for a child. I didn't have it for myself—I didn't want to risk depriving a child of it.

There was a time in my younger life when I had such an insecure sense of myself that all I knew was that I liked to drink coffee and read Charles Dickens. Really. That was all I knew for sure. Everything else was an act. A pretty good one, I'd have to say. I was lucky in that my particular neurosis took the form of striving to make everyone on the planet love me—every cat, dog, waitress, boss, sibling, colleague, teacher, and random person on the subway. Add in a ferocious need to succeed at everything I touched, and I was a pretty high-functioning nut case.

I did not know I was unconditionally beloved. And in that state, no matter what you achieve, it doesn't stick to the ribs. Praise? They didn't really mean it. An Op-Ed in the *Washington Post* yesterday? Yes, but what did I accomplish today? Even the support of my husband, John, whose unconditional love for me never falters, didn't make me well.

Wondrously, things changed. Many years of talk therapy with Betty Ann gradually constructed a self. I came to believe I had the right to my four square feet of oxygen on this earth, and I gradually shed the firm conviction that I was responsible for the world's unhappiness. Thanks to a decade of therapy, I started to become the person I was meant to be, including the mother of two beloved daughters.

Dr. Ottinger and I talked a lot about unconditional love. It is the Rosetta stone of emotional health. If we have it throughout babyhood and early childhood, we are pretty much assured of a sturdy, contented adulthood. If we don't, we'll pay a heavy price for the rest of our lives unless we—or somebody— can rewrite our past.

A friend of mine dragged herself, kicking and screaming, to therapy. Her therapist started at the very beginning and spent months delving into her client's childhood. My friend hated it. She asked me irritably, "Why do we need to talk about childhood? It isn't as if nothing else has happened in my life. Let's get on with it!"

The answer—thank you, Betty Ann—is that who we are and how we navigate life are actually formed in those early years of childhood. The brain literally, physically conforms to our parents' sense of us, and our own sense of ourselves conforms to the brain tracks laid down when we were little. We're not just socialized to believe a certain story about ourselves: the neural pathways in our brains are changed to accommodate that story.

In *Anatomy of the Soul,* Christian psychotherapist Curt Thompson wrote that the story can change:

> Fortunately,...attachment patterns *do* have the capacity
> for change,...but substantial interaction with an outside
> brain relationship or a change in circumstances is
> required for this transformation. We cannot change
> our stories without simultaneously changing the neural
> pathways that correlate with those modifications.

My parents loved my brother and sisters and me, but the parenting norms of the 1950s and their own particular stories were not conducive to undivided individual attention. Thank God, my parents had five of us. We were raised in a benevolent pack. Most of my mother's emotional energy went to my father, and much of his went to his music. We five siblings absorbed our parents' strong work ethic, love of classical music, and robust pride in being Burkhalters.

We also absorbed our mother's single-hearted adoration of her husband, our father. We wanted to be like him, we wanted to please him, and we wanted to be noticed by both of them. Though it was not my parents' intention to teach this, we five learned that attention and recognition are earned by being superb. Superb, after all, is what our dad was and is. As the fourth of five talented kids, I tried my hardest and never believed it was good enough. It wasn't anybody's fault.

I needed a different story, and it took a long time to learn one. I had extraordinarily low self-esteem, was terrified of irritating anyone, and was desperately afraid of failure. I had to go over old ground again and again and again with Dr. Ottinger before that story gradually started to change. I learned how children's emotions developed, and it helped me to be a good parent. I learned how my parents' histories affected them as adults, and that understanding helped me love them more fully and intelligently. I learned about the unexpressed longings each of my siblings had that were so much like mine. I got well.

But here's a puzzle. I did not believe in God during the many years I worked with Dr. Ottinger, and I don't think she was a Christian either. Issues of faith were simply irrelevant. I came to believe in unconditional love—I just didn't know the source of it. And unquestionably, I got better. If God is the source of unconditional love, how did I come to believe in it before I came to believe in him?

The flip side of the puzzle is that Christian believers who are secure in their faith also suffer emotional and psychological illness right along with the rest of the population. Many of my closest Christian friends have benefited greatly from therapy, like I did. In their cases, it worked particularly well because of their underlying trust in God's unconditional love. Other Christians are uniquely disadvantaged because their churches and Christian friends or relatives are hostile to medical or psychological interventions, regarding emotional or mental illness as a lapse of faith.

But in almost all cases, excellent therapy, whether it is with Christian or nonbelieving psychologists and psychiatrists, helps troubled people to heal. How did my secular therapist bring me to a place where I believed myself worthy of unconditional love when neither she nor I believed there was a source for it? Unconditional love isn't just floating on the air. How does something come from nothing? I asked my friend Alex Harris, and he said this: "All truth comes from God. Dr. Ottinger's work with you was successful because it was based on truth. That neither of you believed in God doesn't make the truth of your therapy any less true."

The concept has been around for eons. The psalmist sings:

"The LORD is good to all: and his tender mercies are over all his works.... The LORD upholdeth all that fall, and raiseth up all those that be bowed down.... Thou openest thine hand, and satisfiest the desire of every living thing."

These verses, so well known to mature Christians, hit me like a ton of bricks. This glorious expression of God's love and truth being the source of *everything* that is good, whether it is attributed to the Creator or not, shames the smallness of my understanding of God and my contempt for what I had understood to be the God of the Old Testament. The Lord who "upholdeth all that fall, and raiseth up all those that be bowed down" is a radically generous God, available to all. We here on earth are the ones to confine the Creator in our small circles that include us and those like us and leave the others out.

C. S. Lewis wrote about this very touchingly in the last book of the Chronicles of Narnia, *The Last Battle*. Lewis, one of the most influential Christian thinkers of the twentieth century and, for many, the most articulate defender of the faith, was not what I would call a liberal. Some of his views about women, for example, are typical of his generation and quite awful.

But his concept of a God being greater than the smallness of our vision of him is spectacular. The story—perhaps you know it—is that the Narnians have been in a pitched battle with their historic enemies, the Calormen. The children end up in Narnia-heaven with Aslan. Surprisingly, a young Calormen soldier finds himself there too. He tells Aslan that he had worshiped Tash (the anti-Aslan) and had no right to be there.

Aslan tells the boy that he is welcome, because everything good he had done for Tash, in fact, served Aslan: "For I and he are of such different kinds that no service which is vile can be done to me, and none which is not vile can be done to him."

How radically inclusive is Aslan in stark contrast to many of us human Christians who insist on slicing, dicing, judging, excluding, and codifying. And the overwhelming truth that we are *all* beloved and made in God's image is the most generous of all. I learned that as I talked with my therapist, slowly, slowly, slowly tuning my ear to a different song and unburdening my heavy heart.

For as long as I've known them, my parents were proud, private, and independent. The only things in the world they feared, as near as I can tell, were dementia and nursing homes. In the spring of 2008 my mother moved into a nursing home in Ames, Iowa. She had Alzheimer's and died there four months later.

My mother was virtually orphaned at birth when her mother, Agnes Holland (known as Holly) Mosiman, hemorrhaged and died in a cabin in Saskatchewan, Canada. The premature infant, hastily named after her mother, wasn't expected to live. Her twelve-year-old sister, Leora, wrapped the newborn, placed her in a cigar box, and tucked the little package into a corner of the banked wood stove.

Mom always said that she was the luckiest of the four motherless Mosiman children. Janiece, Eldon, and Leora were sent to live with relatives and worked throughout their childhood. But the baby, Holly, was lovingly raised by her father's two maiden sisters, Ida and Estelle, on the Mosiman farm in southern Ohio.

Theirs was an interesting family. In addition to 'Stell and Ida, it included two older unmarried aunts from among the twelve siblings and my mother's grandparents. They farmed, kept cows and chickens, canned fruit and vegetables, and attended the local Mennonite church. The barn had a haymow. There was a dog named Ole Yeller and another named Pluto. A neighboring farmer named Artie Howe was like one of the family. Ida was a nurse at the nearby steel mill, and 'Stell, who loved classical music, taught piano lessons in town.

When I was a kid, I thought the Mosiman farm was a paradise straight from *Charlotte's Web*. But it wasn't. The family was poor, and the farm work endless. Artie had a tractor accident and lost his arm at the shoulder. And Mom's grandparents gradually became invalids and finally infants. We would call their disease Alzheimer's today. The Mosiman women didn't call it anything in the 1920s and '30s; they simply shouldered this latest burden.

It seems that the women-run family had infinite capacity to absorb the helpless. My mother remembers that her bed-bound and mentally failing grandparents lived for many years, requiring full-time care from 'Stell and Ida. Unmarried or widowed elderly aunts lived at the farm at various times, and Ida and 'Stell cared for them all. Small wonder Mom had a horror of old age and senility.

At the age of forty, Aunt 'Stell married Artie after a decade-long engagement. She had refused to marry until her parents were gone. I don't know why, and my mother doesn't know why. What we do know is that plucky little one-armed Artie faithfully waited for his fiancée. We also know that pregnancies in forty-plus-year-old women have a one-in-thirty chance of resulting in a child with Down syndrome.

And thus it was that Francis Howe was born to the family when Mom was ten years old. He was a much-wanted and much-adored child. That he had a developmental disability was immediately apparent to all but his loving parents, who cherished every hope for their child. As he grew through childhood, he was sent to regular schools, where he learned to read and write. He was passed from grade to grade and graduated from public high school. Because his folks denied his disability, Francis never received any special education or services, nor did he have a chance to meet other kids like himself.

My father told me once how Uncle Artie approached him to help Francis gain admittance to Bluffton College, my par-

ents' alma mater. When Dad told him that there was no possibility of Francis going to college anywhere, ever, Artie was at
first furious and then broke down and wept over his boy.

When I was a child, I always considered Francis to be one
of us kids, although he was a lot stronger than we were. He
carried a bowie knife and worked like a man, muttering under
his breath. Over the years of my childhood, our visits to the
farm became fewer and fewer. Mother told me at the time that
she didn't want us kids to hang out with Francis. She worried
about the muttering and the knife. But she needn't have. He
never hurt any living thing.

Mom left the farm as a teenager to go to school in Cincin-
nati. She lived at a college fraternity house with her aunt Lou-
ise, who was the housemother. My mother expressed no regret
at leaving the farm, but I've always wondered whether her
coolness toward Francis was because he took her place as 'Stell
and Artie's child. Francis stayed. She left.

After high school, Mother went to Bluffton College and
met my father. He was a violinist, conductor, and composer
and a stunningly good-looking man. They fell in love and
married. Our family—five children in nine years—flourished.
But the old farm didn't. First Ida died and then Estelle. Artie
sold the farm, and he and Francis moved into a little house in
Trenton, Ohio. Shortly thereafter, Francis ran away and was
found back at the farm, looking for his mother.

My own mother never looked back. Her connection to

Artie and Francis dwindled after her aunts died. She didn't go to the funeral when Artie died. It must have been frightening for Mom to contemplate taking responsibility for her heart-broken cousin Francis, whom Artie left behind.

Francis became the ward of Hamilton County, Ohio. He was installed at a home for adults with disabilities. I visited him there. It was awful. Thanks to the kindness of a church family who loved Francis and Artie, an alternative was found. Francis moved into a small group home, and he lived there until his death just a few months before my mother died.

Mental disability and mental illness. It is such a wide strand in the fabric of my family. The loneliness and suffering of people like Francis and my grandmother Adah and millions like them used to be evidence to me of an absent God. If any creatures on this earth can be said to have been abandoned by God, it is people with mental disabilities. Loathed, feared, and abused in every era, adults and children with mental illnesses and developmental disabilities appear to be evidence of a cruel world and an indifferent Creator.

It wasn't until I became a Christian that I learned, to my joy, that Jesus loved crazy people. Every one of the Gospels reports that everywhere Jesus went, he would seek out and heal people with mental disabilities. My favorite is the schizophrenic man who lived in the tombs in the region of the Gerasenes. This pitiful outcast had been repeatedly chained, hand and foot, but he tore the chains apart and broke the irons on his ankles. Night and day among the tombs and in the hills he would scream and cut himself with stones.

When the man sees Jesus from a distance, he runs down from the tombs and falls to his knees before him. In what must be one of the most poignant scenes in the Bible, this man, who is so feared by his neighbors that he's chained and shackled, so isolated that he lives among the dead, and in such pain that he mutilates himself, begs Jesus not to torture him.

Jesus asks a question that the insane man has probably never heard before. "What is your name?"

Heartbreakingly, this schizophrenic homeless man, who only knows himself as several selves, answers, "My name is Legion; for we are many." Curiously, he begs Jesus not to send "them" out of the area.

Scripture refers to "them" as the demons that have taken possession of Legion and are speaking through him to Jesus. The same story in the gospel of Luke actually has the demons themselves begging Jesus not to send them away. Luke's version also states that it was the demons that drove Legion into the wilds.

Somehow I doubt it. I'll bet money that the good folk of the Gerasenes *themselves* hounded the desperately ill man and his multiple personality "demons" into hiding among the tombstones. Having been exiled and bound in chains, Legion is a man who knows something about torture, and he obviously fears that Jesus will inflict more of it on him. Thus he begs Jesus again and again not to send "them," meaning him, out of the area, or "into the abyss," as Luke reports. Demon possession was a metaphor for mental illness, of course.

What follows is surpassingly bizarre. A herd of two thousand pigs is standing by, handily. Legion's demons beg Jesus to send them into the pigs. He agrees. The spirits come out of Legion, inhabit the pigs, and the whole herd gallops over the abyss, falls into a lake, and drowns. The people who had gathered demand that Jesus leave. Chained and raving lunatic? Suicidal pigs? Deal-making demons? Go. Just go.

I don't have an explanation for the pigs, and festive though they be, they aren't the most important part of the story. The best part is where Legion puts on clothes and sits at Jesus's feet and begs to accompany him. Now here is a place I'd like to do a little creative editing of the gospel. Don't you just long for Jesus to invite Legion to come with him? He must have been Legion's first friend. I think Legion would have made a fine disciple, adding a nice touch of diversity to the group.

Jesus has other plans for him, though. "Go home to your friends, and tell them how much the Lord has done for you, and what mercy he has shown you." Jesus, apparently, wishes to have his good deed proclaimed by the man who benefited from it.

Having an infamous and much-feared psychotic as your messenger is a bit of a gamble, don't you think? Jesus might just as easily have asked some bystander or one of his disciples to tell the story. He didn't. He asked Legion to tell his own story in his own words. Mark reports that Legion did as he was asked. "And everyone was amazed."

Once again, I'm fall-down amazed myself at Jesus's incredible courage and love for people whom normal folks hate and fear. By befriending Legion, Jesus got himself disinvited from the community. People with mental illnesses or developmental disabilities to this day are the most wretched of the earth. But they, too, are made in God's image, and like all of us, they need healing.

Dutch priest and scholar Henri Nouwen wrote an extraordinary book about the meaning of mental disability in God's creation. It is based on his seven years as a caregiver at L'Arch Daybreak community for a man with profound mental and physical disabilities. Nouwen was familiar with mental illness, suffering himself from depression and a crippling need for affirmation and love. Nearing a mental and spiritual breakdown, he joined the Toronto-based community as a respite from his globe-circling speaking and teaching schedule.

Caring for Adam Arnett, who was nonverbal and largely immobile, appears to have been an epiphany for Nouwen. He wrote in *Adam, God's Beloved:*

If people knew us as we really are, without all the
worldly decorations we have gathered, would they still
love us?... This is the central question of identity: Are
we good because of what we do or have, or because of
who we are? Am I somebody because the world makes
me into somebody or am I somebody because I belonged to God long before I belonged to the world?

My friend Laurie Ahern, who is a disability rights activist,
told me that her son Josh experienced unconditional love when
he volunteered in a L'Arch community of people with developmental disabilities in Massachusetts. "He told me he loved the
residents because they never judged him: they didn't know
how. They only loved him and let him know straightaway if
anything was wrong."

Nouwen concluded that Adam was God's gift to him and
to the world, given to teach him how to love and receive love
unconditionally. I think that this is what Francis was to Uncle
Artie and Aunt 'Stell. I think this was also true for my father
when Mom's mind began to slip away.

My mother's mental capacity began to diminish a long
time ago. It happened slowly, and it wasn't linear. She would
be herself for a long time; then she'd say something odd or act
peculiarly; then she was back to normal. My sisters and brother
and I couldn't figure her out. There would be times when she

was quite irritated at us for no reason, but mostly she seemed happy, sitting in her chair with a pile of books. Over the years, she left the house less and less and, without calling any notice to it, stopped cooking, driving, and grocery shopping.

My father quietly picked up all the things that Mother used to do. The grandkids' Christmas presents were chosen and wrapped by Dad. He cleaned the house, made the meals, and in the last several years of Mom's life, selected her clothes and helped her dress. My father was so protective of Mom's dignity that he covered for her in social settings. We five kids didn't really know how much Mother's mental capacity had deteriorated because Dad would slip her cues, finish her sentences, and suavely redirect her when she became confused.

The radically beautiful thing about all this is that Laurence Burkhalter is not a particularly patient man. He does not suffer fools gladly, and he has a fairly well-developed distaste for clutter, filth, and stupidity. Talking with your mouth full would inspire a curt correction or glare from Dad during family dinners. We all still twitch like we've been tasered when some grandchild at the dinner table, oblivious to the Burkhalter rules, slurps their glass of milk or chews audibly.

Yet this is the man who laundered the clothes Mother soiled when cancer had destroyed her bowel control, cleaned up the floor after accidents, and listened attentively to her rambling remarks. As Mother became increasingly vague and helpless, my father became more patient and kind. He never asked for help, and he turned aside my admiring comments about his care for her.

At one of the last family gatherings before Mom died, she was sitting quietly across the living room from Dad at my sister Karol's farmhouse. Talk and laughter swirled among their five kids, in-laws, and grandchildren. Mother seemed lost in her own world, but Dad kept close watch over her. At one point, I saw him get up from his chair, cross the room, and softly rearrange her rumpled hair. Then he went back to his seat. It was an unremarkable, little, obsessive-compulsive gesture, but so tender that I had to turn away to hide my tears.

Paul Tillich, the German theologian who tried to make sense of God in a world gone mad during the Holocaust, wrote about the meaning of divine Providence. Tillich discarded the notion that divine Providence means everything bad will eventually turn out right: things don't. And trust in divine Providence does not mean there is hope in every situation: there is often not. Alzheimer's, for example, is a bitch. So is cancer. (I said that, not Tillich.)

Rather, he wrote, "Providence means that there is a creative and saving possibility implied in every situation, which cannot be destroyed by any event." And he found this saving possibility at the worst time in human history:

When death rains from heaven as it does now, when cruelty wields power over nations and individuals as it does now, when hunger and persecution drive millions from place to place as they do now, and when prisons and slums all over the world distort the humanity of the bodies and souls of men as they do now—we can boast in that time, and just in that time, that even all of this can not separate us from the love of God.

Jesus's kindness was Tillich's "saving possibility" for Legion's tormented, tragic life. I have to remember that we don't get to see it as vividly in our lives, because Jesus simply isn't here. But believing that there *is* a possibility of some higher goodness in all situations has allowed me to think about the world differently and to start to reconcile the polar opposites of a loving God and a wretched earth.

ten

The Selfish Gene

I came out of my Capitol Hill row house one summer day with Fala on a leash and saw my good neighbor Rita wearing splints for carpal tunnel syndrome on both arms and a face mask as she usually does. She was industriously whacking bushes in Sis Allen's front yard. Sis is an ancient lady who lives by herself a few doors down from me. I stopped to say hi.

Rita hung out at Sis's place a lot those days. On Wednesday and Sunday mornings she'd walk Sis across the street to church. She and a couple other Samaritans did Sis's laundry, picked up prescriptions, took her to the doctor.

Sis had had a heart attack—her second. When she came home from the hospital, her tremor was so pronounced she could scarcely hold a cup, much less manipulate the inhaler that delivers one of her twenty prescription meds. Her heart and kidneys are failing, and she has the worst diet I've ever seen in a human being, adult or child. Sis eats almost nothing except McDonald's burgers, diet soda, and chocolate.

Sis asked me to pick up some groceries for her: a package of hamburger buns. In that officious tone I can't suppress when I'm with Sis, I said, "How about some grapes? How about some cheese? Apples?"

She answered, with revulsion, "Nah. I don't need that stuff. I got my chocolate." She sure did. Two huge Hershey's bars, a well-stocked M&M's machine, two monstrous brownies, and a box of chocolate doughnuts.

I shuddered. Sick elderly people are not supposed to scarf down McNuggets and Tastykakes. No wonder she had had two heart attacks. She has lived in her dark, tiny row house for eighty years, and it looks it. Mounds of old mail and magazines are piled on the coffee table; hundreds of snapshots cover every inch of the refrigerator and cabinets. Three dozen mechanical stuffed animals occupy the bulk of the seating space on the couch.

I made the mistake of stopping by to visit Sis one evening when Rita was there, watching *Jeopardy*. Rita was happy to see me, because she was leaving the following morning to spend the next three weeks taking care of her elderly father in Wisconsin. She had been dropping in on Sis every day at 8:00 in the morning and 8:00 at night to help her with her medication. How handy that a neighbor who lived much closer (that would be me) was available to take over the job!

I really did not want to do this. I prefer to exercise my compassion more generally. I'll write about it, for example. And I love the idea of loving my neighbor. I think about it all the time! But I do find that sick and needy *abstract* people are much more attractive than *actual* sick and needy people who live only two hundred yards from me. Ironic isn't it? I do human rights work for a living and have a three-decade history of being pretty good at it. But human rights policy—my specialty—has absolutely nothing to do with my personally being a good neighbor.

When Rita proposed to pass the good neighbor torch to me, I looked around frantically for alternatives. There were none. It turns out that the idea of the Good Neighbor doesn't actually help an old lady wrestle her medication out of well-armored blister packs or pick up a case of Ensure. It never watches *Wheel of Fortune* with her.

It needed to be me. Except that I wasn't a Good Neighbor like Rita. I was more of a Bad Neighbor, faking it. I wanted to be the kind of person whose heart had been transformed so that being a good neighbor would simply come naturally. It didn't. I had to gird my loins twice a day to visit the house and mentally slap myself to stay with Sis beyond the minimum required to get her up, find her hearing aids, and open her medicine.

It's hard to be in a relationship with someone you didn't choose. My reluctance to go, every single time, reminds me that I've surrounded myself with people I love—people who are interesting. Intellectuals. Vegetarians. Daughters. Clean-cut colleagues. Not one of them in Depends.

I was disgusted at how little I had changed over those months of trying to be a Good Neighbor to Sis. Jesus asked me to love exactly one person outside my charmed circle, and I was not doing it well. I woke up at two o'clock one night with this question on my mind: *How long do I have to do this?*

I popped open a beer and leafed through the Bible for the story of the Good Samaritan. To be honest, it wasn't that much help. As you know, a poor Jew is set upon by thieves, beaten to a pulp, and left for dead. Two religious leaders, who should have helped the victim, instead leave him where he lies on the road. A Samaritan—a member of a despised ethnic minority—binds up the man's wounds, puts him on his own donkey, and takes him to an inn. He leaves instructions and money for his care and promises to return to repay anything additional that might be spent to aid the victim.

I like the Good Samaritan as well as the next person, but here's the thing: *he got to leave.* The Good Samaritan left the beaten-up guy in the care of others and got on his donkey and rode away. My neighbor Sis is permanently here, in a row house three down from mine. She is getting more frail, deaf, and obstinate by the day. She falls frequently but refuses to wear one of those emergency buttons around her neck. She sits in the dark to save electricity, and she still gives me a heck of a bad time when I don't put things away as she would.

I lived three houses down from Sis for almost thirty years without offering more than a hello when we met on the street or when resetting her clocks at daylight savings time. When she needed me, I signed up for only one reason: I did what I did not want to do because I hated not doing it more.

I learned a little about the meaning of obedience, though. We think that love is an emotion, and sometimes it is. But doing what Jesus asked when you don't want to is a truer example of obedience. I was very obedient throughout my childhood. I never wanted anyone to be mad at me or find fault. I did everything I was asked by my parents and by every boss I had from the time I got a job as a waitress at sixteen until today. But I managed to avoid Jesus's instructions to love my neighbor for most of my lifetime. Even as a new believer, I did not want to do what I knew was right.

I prayed every single day that I might be able to love Sis as she loves me—and like she loves everyone. I wondered if dragging my useless self over to her house without love was worth anything at all. I did my best, and it was crap.

I went over there one day and was almost knocked over by the urine smell. The source was an open garbage can in the kitchen that was half-full of used Depends. I located a box of clean garbage bags and commenced to haul the Depends stash out of the can with alacrity.

Sis hollered at me: "Leave that alone! It's not full yet."

I hollered back: "Well, it doesn't smell very nice, Sis."

Sis: "I don't smell anything."

Me, in a louder, more deliberate tone: "Well, I do. It really smells in here."

At which point in the dialogue, Sis wilted and said in a subdued voice: "Oh. I didn't know. I can't smell it because I live here."

Oh, way to go, Holly! What would Jesus *not* do? Humiliate an aged and fragile woman who simply wants to live her life the way she has always done: frugally and independently. In a rare moment of clarity, I mentally observed the fact that I am indeed a fool and started to back-pedal. I told Sis that my house smells like dirty dog (which it does) and that everybody can smell it except the people who live there. She reluctantly let me bag up the trash, and next morning I snuck in a couple extra boxes of garbage bags when she wasn't looking.

Oddly, from that moment it became easier to be Sis's Good Neighbor. Something about seeing her stripped to the bare bone with her dignity affronted made me more patient and kind.

I'm not quite sure why occasionally we are given intimate glimpses into another's suffering, but I do know that it's vital to act on them.

A particular memory of a little girl nicknamed "Witchy" in my first-grade class at a country school torments me to this day. She was very poor—literally dressed in rags—and her hair was matted and dirty. She didn't have lunch one day, and another girl teased her for it. Witchy cried. If only she hadn't cried.

I was six years old, and I did not help. But I remember that little girl's hunger and humiliation as if it had happened to me, and I'm going to wince in pain for the rest of my life for failing to comfort her. I think that it is Witchy, even more than God or Rita, who got me over to Sis's house. A pail full of wet Depends is chicken feed compared to the remorse and regret I would feel for the rest of my life if I didn't respond to Sis's loneliness and need.

It was remorse that started those daily trips to Sis's house, but something like love that kept me going there, long after Rita returned to Capitol Hill to resume Sis patrol. When I arrived, Sis was usually watching a TV divorce show and simultaneously doing word searches. Her lips moved as her pen scrawled shakily across the page. Sis said that Jesus helped her find the words. We would watch a little TV, open the mail, and I would make bologna sandwiches for the next day. She'd fill me in on news from the neighborhood and ask about my girls.

That was four years ago. Sis is now ninety-three and in the last months of her life. There are nurses with her and a hospital bed in her cramped little house. My heart breaks to see that Sis can't even be tempted to take a bite from a McDouble. All she eats now are one or two M&M's. She wheezes when she breathes, and she can't get comfortable in her chair or see well enough to do word searches.

But her face lights up when I come through the door. I sit on a windup bear on the sofa and hold her hand. She's anxious to hear about everybody's health, and she has some candy she wants me to take home to the girls. And I'm glad. I have slogged along these past four years, doing what Jesus asked me to do for Sis. And obedience changed my heart so that now it isn't a duty anymore.

Thank you, Sis. Thank you for waiting for me.

Sis was a hugely important teacher in my early years of living in faith. There were other teachers too. One of them was my heart, which was supposed to work flawlessly until I'm ninety-six years old and go floating off to bake cookies with Jesus. I trusted this outcome because I am maniacally disciplined about my health.

About fifteen years ago a close friend died of bone cancer. It really, truly could have been me. She left behind young kids. I decided on the day she died that I would do absolutely every-thing in my power to lower the odds of dying young. Cancer is pretty random, but heart disease, the number-one killer of American women, is largely preventable.

I became the poster child for not having heart disease. I stopped eating meat, jogged, and took an aspirin every day to prevent clots. One fine day five years ago, I noticed that my chest hurt when I took Fala out for her 6:00 a.m. walk to the park. Must have been too much coffee on an empty stomach. A few days later, I noticed I was panting when I walked up-stairs. No worries there—I have such bad anxiety, I'm breath-less most of the time. As the days went by, my chest would hurt a little more, and I'd cut Fala's walk short by a couple more blocks.

When it got to the point that I had to stop and sit down in the middle of the sidewalk when Fala and I had walked for only a few minutes, it seemed time to check in with a doctor. Naturally it took a week and a half to get an appointment, but one thing led to another, and I eventually found myself trot-ting on a treadmill at the cardiologist's office. I got a clue that things were not as they should be when my cardiologist took a look at the EKG ribbon, stopped the machine, sat me down, and put a nitroglycerin tablet under my tongue.

It seems I had a total blockage of the left anterior descending artery. The doctors call it the "widow maker." We feminist gals can call it the "widower maker," but you get the point. This is one badass artery when it gets choked up.

The cardiologist himself walked me across the street to the hospital, and the next morning a catheter was snaked up through the femoral artery in my groin and a stent installed in the blockage. Other than epic bruising from the procedure, things seemed fine, and I was home within two days. But three days later I was back in the hospital catheter lab for a second angioplasty and stent to open a different artery that had hemorrhaged during the first procedure and had a long, ugly blood clot in it.

Now I had epic bruising on both thighs and was beginning to find all of this a lot less fun than you might think. A low moment came when a senior cardiologist told me he'd never seen a case like mine in his entire career. I had always wanted to be a prodigy but definitely not this kind.

I learned a few things on this journey. I learned that extravagantly divesting myself of every vice didn't protect me from heart disease. I learned that I don't control the world. I learned how vain I was about being healthy. I learned that my habit of juggling too much, too fast, for too long might just kill me someday. Basically, I learned that self-sufficiency is a big, fat con job.

There is a story told by both Matthew and Luke about Jesus healing the servant of a Roman centurion. "When [Jesus] entered Capernaum, a centurion came to him, appealing to him and saying, 'Lord, my servant is lying at home paralyzed, in terrible distress.' And he said to him, 'I will come and cure him.' The centurion answered, 'Lord, I am not worthy to have you come under my roof; but only speak the word, and my servant will be healed.'"

Then the centurion adds this description of himself: "For I also am a man under authority, with soldiers under me; and I say to one, 'Go,' and he goes, and to another, 'Come,' and he comes, and to my slave, 'Do this,' and the slave does it." I can relate to the centurion. Oh, not the part about people obeying me. I can't get the dog to obey me unless I've got a pepperoni treat in my hand, much less get humans to come and go on command. No, what I relate to is the centurion's self-reliance. He obeys orders smartly, and people under his command know what to do, and the sun rises and falls predictably. A well-ordered life in a well-ordered world.

To paraphrase the centurion, I tell myself, "Go," and I go. I tell myself, "Do this," and I do it. I am a woman under orders: mine. But when I ordered my heart to work well, it didn't. It isn't under my control, and neither is much of life, no matter how many spinning plates I can keep in the air.

Why is it that we humans, me and most everybody else, find it so hard to acknowledge that there is a source of sufficiency beyond ourselves? As my friend Christine Britton says, "How come I have to do things my way four thousand times, failing every single time, before I remember to pray for help?"

In the second chapter of G. K. Chesterton's Christian apologia *Orthodoxy*, a madman epitomizes the person utterly unconscious of God. The "lunatic" in Chesterton's essay is a surrogate for the rational humanist or atheist. Chesterton portrays this person as one whose self-sufficiency is so complete that contemplation of the eternal is neither desired nor possible.

I don't much enjoy Chesterton's insults to the insane, but he's onto something. The "lunatic" in the nineteenth-century asylum whose entire reality was in his head is not, in spiritual terms, all that different from me or you or any other busy, bustling, self-absorbed person who wakes up every day and thinks we're at the center of the world and in charge of it, from our first cup of coffee in the morning to the pillows on our bed at night.

For fifty years I stayed busy and productive enough to avoid thinking about all kinds of things, most especially about my smallness, the world's vastness, and what the hell we're doing here. But the point where one's tiny scrabblings simply can't supply the meaning and grounding that human beings yearn for can be the moment that your heart and mind start to make room for a new idea. The idea that there is a source of goodness and beauty outside of me-myself-and-I that is infinitely large, infinitely generous, and infinitely available.

We are not sufficient. That one true thing became clear to me during my heart-attack drama. My misbehaving heart and I needed to live differently, and I didn't know what to do. And to be honest, my doctors didn't know either. Nobody seemed to understand why I'd had the blockages or how to prevent their recurrence. Worse, my chest ached for months after the stent procedures, but two different sets of cardiologists told me that the pain was psychosomatic.

Marvelous. You tell your doctor that you take meds for anxiety, and the next thing you know the actual angina you're feeling in your heart (exactly like the pain that put me in the hospital) is phantom. The only one of my doctors who *didn't* think the chest pain was all in my head was my psychiatrist.

I was desperately frightened for the better part of a year. I only felt safe when I was in the cardiologist's office. I wanted to have an angiogram every month, just to make sure nothing had gone south since the last one. After about six months of this, my cardiologist said quite bluntly, "There's nothing wrong with you. Go see your regular doctor. I can't do anything else for you."

I got a new cardiologist. Several different ones. They all said the same thing, albeit more kindly than the one who kicked me out of his office. "You're fine. You couldn't possibly be having chest pain." I just didn't know what to do. I have never felt more helpless in my life. I had tried so hard to be healthy, and it hadn't worked. I was every bit as vulnerable as my friend who had died of cancer.

I prayed, but not for my arteries. I can't explain this, but I think it's cheesy and foolish to pray for my arteries. There are many arteries in the world that are in worse shape than mine—Jesus, go fix those. This is confusing for me right now. When I pray for patience and love and generosity, those prayers are answered. So if God can hear my prayer and heal my character, why can't prayer heal my arteries? I don't know, but I'm not going to pray for my arteries.

But I did pray for something else. I desperately needed God's help in healing my hyperactivity, anxiety, self-absorption, and most of all, my fear. I don't know why I think God cares more about my fear than my arteries, but I do.

About a year after the heart attack, I was walking with Fala in the park, clutching my chest and wondering if I was having another when I stopped walking and thought, *What am I supposed to do, Jesus?* The Lord never talks to me, but I'm telling you, that prayer was answered as surely as if he'd taken out a bullhorn and bellowed into my ear, because the next day, as I was poking around in a bookstore in the health section, there in front of me was the answer: *Prevent and Reverse Heart Disease,* by Caldwell Esselstyn.

Dr. Esselstyn is a prominent doctor in his seventies who

has been working for twenty years with patients whose hearts were so bad they were literally sitting around, waiting to die. The stents and bypasses that pass for cardiology care in our country had run their course, and these folks were goners. Except they weren't. Dr. Esselstyn persuaded them to immediately change their diet to a plant-based, whole-grain, nonfat regimen. Those who stuck to it got well. Their chest pain disappeared, and their arteries cleared out. Really. He's got before-and-after angiograms to prove it.

I was already a vegetarian, so I decided to go the whole distance. I cut out all animal food (giving up cheese still grieves me) as well as most refined flour. Basically, I ate what Dr. Esselstyn said to eat, and within three weeks my chest pain vanished. As a person with anxiety as well as heart disease, I suppose I have to consider that my chest pain—and its eradication—was psychosomatic, but I don't think so. The science of nutrition, I learned from Dr. Esselstyn and others, is well established: fat, meat, and refined grains are killing us. Animal products can and do damage arteries, and they made my chest hurt. When I eat carefully, I feel like a million bucks. Did I mention that beer is allowed on the Esselstyn diet? Thank you, Jesus.

Our bodies betray each and every one of us, eventually and inevitably. As my pal Anne Weaver, who is about eighty, whispered loudly when I saw her recently, "Old age sucks. Pass the word to your friends." I'm fifty-nine and I feel it. But I'm not scared anymore. I asked for wisdom, and Jesus showed up, dragging Caldwell Esselstyn in tow. I am very grateful.

When the shit hits the fan, I eat junk—including pork, which I happen to love, and doughnuts. But I have this built-in truth button: my chest starts to hurt after a few days of debauchery. I reluctantly say good-bye to cheese, ice cream, and ham and go back to garbanzos, soy milk, and broccoli.

I wish I could deal as straightforwardly with the anxiety and stress that are the likelier cause of my heart problems. I am wired for anxiety, and even though I take terrific medications, I'm still me. I need to change more than my diet. I desperately need to believe that I don't have to earn love, that I don't need to be perfect, that I'm good enough, including when I fail.

I'm not getting there on my own. *Lord, I am not worthy to receive you, but only say the word, and I shall be healed.*

About five years ago at Christmastime, my siblings and I were sitting around the dining room table at Roo's home after a huge meal and arguing about Christianity. I held down the God fort with my brother, Gary, a Lutheran pastor, while Roo and Karol lobbed questions and dissected answers. Kathy wandered between the two camps, attempting to make peace. Things got so intense that my daughter Grace, listening in from the sidelines, beetled off in search of a grownup. I heard her bellow in the distance, "Daaaad! Mom's fighting about God again!"

I hated that fight. I was very new to faith and didn't defend it very well. Karol had this aggressive way of firing unanswerable questions at me. I was trying to defend Jesus's divinity at one point, and she interrupted to ask, with exaggerated interest, "And what about *Mary*?"

Roo, taking the intellectual high ground, said, "As Bertrand Russell says, 'I'm not interested in the questions that Christianity is supposed to answer.'"

Well, *fine,* you pagan snots. It was an easy argument for them because they weren't defending anything. If I'd had any brains I would have turned the questions on them: "Well, what do you believe? Everybody has to believe in something." But no, I had to take offense on Jesus and Mary's behalf, raise my voice, and scare the children and pets.

Nowadays, however, I am more comfortable in my new skin, and I'm more comfortable talking calmly about issues of faith, especially with Karol.

Karol is smart and thoughtful, a Unitarian and a secular humanist. One of the issues that Karol and I chewed on recently was whether human kindness is innate or whether it reflects a source beyond and above us, namely, God. She argues that human kindness, collaboration, and generosity are hard-wired into the human species over our millennia on earth by a process of natural selection. At the dawn of the age of *Homo sapiens*, people had to live in groups and help each other or they would have perished. Violent individualists died out. Those who survived to pass on their genes were those who cooperated, nurtured, and shared. God doesn't account for human goodness; evolution does.

A good example of the evolution of gentleness can be seen in greyhounds. These lovely creatures have been bred over hundreds of years to race in packs. If one of them is aggressive and attacks another member of the pack, the hunt goes to hell. Such dogs are immediately destroyed. It happens to this very day. And as a consequence, aggression has largely been selected out of the breed. Greyhounds are timid and quiet. There are dozens of greyhounds in my neighborhood that have been rescued from the track. I've never heard one bark or seen one go after another dog. (A rabbit is another story, of course.)

Applied to people, I guess it would go something like this: violent, antisocial individuals are disruptive to communities and families that are required to raise human young. Perhaps such individuals are weeded out by natural selection—like wars, hunting accidents, and violent crime. Social norms against predators are found in virtually all societies throughout history, although I don't actually think this selection process makes humans any less violent.

But there is a chillier version of societal natural selection, most prominently articulated by scientist Richard Dawkins, author of *The Selfish Gene.* His worldview goes like this:

> In a universe of electrons and selfish genes, blind physical forces and genetic replication, some people are going to get hurt, other people are going to get lucky, and you won't find any rhyme or reason in it, nor any justice. The universe that we observe has precisely the properties we should expect if there is, at bottom, no design, no purpose, no evil, no good, nothing but pitiless indifference.

I never thought about any of this before believing in God. And now, I'm no creationist, but I don't share either the positive or negative implications of Darwinism when it comes to human morality. Karol's theory about kindness contributing to the survival of the fittest just doesn't explain our species' proclivity for war, torture, and murder. And, at the opposite end of the spectrum, Dawkins's selfish genes and pitiless indifference can't account for my friend Laurie Ahern.

Laurie is a courageous and beautiful fifty-nine-year-old and the president of Disability Rights International. DRI is a small, crusading, international human rights organization that investigates abuses against people with mental illnesses and developmental disabilities. Laurie and her colleagues go searching in the world's darkest corners for adults and children who appear to have been abandoned by all, including God. Truly, institutions that confine those with mental illnesses or developmental disabilities are the inner circle of hell. The inmates are tormented, starved, humiliated, and tied. They are considered a subspecies, and the abuses they suffer are the worst I have seen in my life. Because these atrocities take place in medical or psychiatric institutions, society assumes there is a medical reason for the conditions in which these people live and die. There isn't.

The glorious good news is that things are changing. Thanks to Laurie and DRI, institutions in Serbia and Kosovo, where mentally ill women were routinely raped, have been closed and the residents relocated to group homes. Paraguayan teenage boys who were literally kept naked in metal cages for most of their lives have been released to loving foster care. A brilliant international treaty on the rights of people with disabilities has been adopted, and DRI's recommendations on the rights of adults and children with mental disabilities are included.

To do this work requires courage and love on an order that I can barely imagine. Like firefighters, DRI staff members enter places of horror and darkness and danger that everyone else flees. They do so because helpless people will die unless someone finds them and gets them out. Laurie Ahern's courage and love are even more miraculous because she herself has suffered some of the abuses she is investigating. She is the human rights version of a firefighter who suffered third-degree burns over her entire body when her home burned down around her and yet keeps heading straight back into the flames to rescue others.

When she was eighteen years old, Laurie experienced a psychotic break as a consequence of many years of childhood sexual abuse. She was forcibly confined in a psychiatric institution. There, a psychiatrist sexually abused her. Miraculously, and in spite of medical professionals, Laurie got well. When she got out of the hospital, she lived with various friends and joined a battered women's group. She had been battered as a kid and battered by life, and she didn't know how to cope. She wasn't given help from psychiatrists. She got it from those women, from friends. Laurie had a son and raised him to become a fine man, and she became the leading advocate for people with mental disabilities in the United States. Now, she's taken her gifts and her courage and put them to work globally.

A couple of years ago, Laurie and DRI founder Eric Rosenthal were investigating abuses against people with mental disabilities in a Turkish psychiatric institution. They were on an official tour with the hospital medical director when Laurie murmured a word to Eric and slipped away from their minder. She quietly left the hospital and headed toward another building that was most definitely not on the tour.

It was a dark, barren structure, with broken windows on

the first floor. Passing it previously, Laurie thought it was deserted until she saw a face at a barred second-floor window. Determined to get to those people, she squeezed through a broken window and landed in a pitch-dark room with inches of standing water on the floor. Laurie groped her way to the stairs and made her way to the upper floors.

And there she found a world of stunning degradation. Emaciated children unable to feed themselves were starving in their cribs. Adults and children were tied to beds and cribs in four-point restraints. Children who were scratching and mutilating themselves from sheer lack of any physical or mental stimulation had large plastic bottles permanently taped over their hands. There was no training, no exercise, no nursing care.

Laurie and Eric's visit turned into a two-year investigation of psychiatric institutions in Turkey. They discovered that staff routinely administered unmodified electric shock, without anesthesia or medication, to the brains of developmentally disabled children—an ignorant practice with no medical precedent. It seemed to be for the purpose of quieting unruly inmates; in reality it was torture. When they publicized their findings, there was an outpouring of outrage in Turkey and around the world. The Turkish government responded with a sustained and serious campaign to end the abuses. The practice of unmodified electroconvulsive shock was stopped entirely, the institutions were closed, and the inmates were relocated to more humane facilities.

In Richard Dawkins's world of no inherent good, no evil, no pity, no courage, and no God, those mentally and physically disabled Turkish children have no value whatsoever. There would be no DRI to find them and no international outcry when the conditions of their confinement were exposed. There wouldn't be any rationale for the Turkish government to spend resources to better their lives.

I get Dawkins's theory, and I think it is rational. There is as much evidence on this earth of randomness and cruelty as there is of goodness. I didn't believe in God precisely because I couldn't see evidence of overarching goodness in this mess we live in on earth. But I believe now that Dawkins is wrong. I think he's wrong because I also see evidence that human beings appear to be hard-wired to experience some degree of discomfort when we experience the suffering of others. Every human culture and society has a sense of fundamental right and wrong, of justice and injustice, and certain bedrock moral precepts are common to them all.

In *Mere Christianity*, C. S. Lewis stated that all creatures are bound by physical laws that they are not free to disobey—gravitation, heredity, the laws of chemistry. Humans are the only species to be subject to a law that they may choose to disobey: the law of nature—morality. He wrote:

These, then, are the two points I wanted to make. First, that human beings, all over the earth, have this curious idea that they ought to behave in a certain way, and cannot really get rid of it. Secondly, that they do not in fact behave in that way. They know the Law of Nature; they break it.

It takes a Laurie Ahern to bring what is hidden into the light and to remind us of our humanity when we are horrified by the treatment of our fellow creatures by our fellow creatures. It happens that neither Laurie nor Eric is a Christian. That fact in no way alters my conviction that the love and courage to fight for and save the naked, shivering, terrified Paraguayan teenagers in a cage and the Auschwitz-thin Turkish child with bottles over his hands come from a source outside our small selves.

As my friend Alex told me, all truth comes from God. Laurie and Eric's truth that these children and adults are beloved and valuable is God's truth. Their heart and courage are God's answer to the gross injustices and abuses suffered by the least of these, those made in his image whom he loves. And the atrocities? Where do they come from? They come from us. We are made in a good God's image, but we're free to disfigure ourselves into something ghastly—and do so in small and large ways all the time. Which means that, as Richard Dawkins would have it, human beings are perfectly capable of being pitiless, unjust, and grotesquely cruel, and at various points in history we turn the earth into a charnel house. But Dawkins and I part company over the question of whether this is the best we've got and the best we can do.

The conviction that there is a source for goodness beyond ourselves is another precious discovery from living in faith. It gives me a different way to look at the world that brings me great joy. And that's just the truth of it. When I think of Laurie and Eric and all those who love the least of these as being partners (sometimes unwitting partners) in a great plan, of which we only know a tiny piece, it gives me hope that there is such a thing as a kingdom of God and that if we look carefully, we get to see it unfold on this earth with our own eyes.

When I started working at International Justice Mission, I was intimidated by the interns. The organization has about one hundred new ones every year. Many go abroad to work in our foreign offices, and some stay back at headquarters, where I am. They all appear to be cheerful young Christians, well educated, well spoken, and, of course, wearing the IJM uniform: boring dark suits.

The interns all seem to have grown up in Christian families. They "came to Jesus" at the age of eight, became counselors at Young Life summer camp, and they know Bible verses as well as they know their home addresses. The phrase "happy-clappy Christians" could have been invented for them.

It is precisely the idea that Christians have it all figured out that is so irritating to nonbelievers. We skeptics and doubters turn a jaundiced eye on these scrubbed and wholesome college kids and think, grimly, *Wait until you get mugged by life.*

After seven years at IJM, I've come to know a lot of young Christians, and I've learned that my assumptions and prejudices about them were insufferably wrong. Everybody has a story, and for many of our young interns, that story has included suffering, loss, doubt, and struggle.

Several times a year, IJM's senior staff spend a day with each new class of interns. We break into small groups, and everyone shares something of their own faith journey and what brought them to International Justice Mission.

One young woman, whom one might have assumed was a happy-clappy Christian, told her story in a soft and steady voice. She got pregnant in high school and had a baby girl. She didn't marry the baby's father, though the two of them tried to raise her together. But their beautiful daughter was born with profound disabilities that even the best doctors couldn't fix. The little lass lived for ten months, and her young parents loved her. Then she died.

Our intern said quietly that she had to believe in God,

because without him, she would not have been able to endure the grief. That lovely young woman stayed on to work at IJM for about a year after her internship ended; then she returned home to enroll in nursing school.

I make no secret with our interns of my own struggles in life and in faith, especially my battle with heart disease and anxiety disorder. And that opens a door to conversations I never expected to have at IJM. One young woman worries terribly about her mother, who is an alcoholic. Another intern has been bulimic for ten years and doesn't know what to do. Many of these kids have parents or close relatives with serious mental illness, and almost all of them, like any person of faith, have had periods of spiritual drought where they doubted everything they ever knew about God.

At the end of one semester, one of our most successful interns, a poised, smart, and beautiful young woman, asked if she could talk to me. She came to my office, sat a bit, then said, "I've lost my faith." We talked a little while, and she told me about how she had believed in God throughout her childhood but had lost her faith in high school when her beloved pastor and spiritual mentor betrayed her trust in him.

The young woman fixed me with a long, sober look and asked, "Why do you believe in God at all?" It was a bad moment. I'm not much for evangelizing and know too little of Scripture. I prefer jokes to salvation stories, and I heartily wished there were a grownup in the room who could offer this intelligent and serious young woman some hope. I've got my own doubts! Why me?

I thought for a while. And then I told her the only thing I know. Why do I believe in God? Because of prayer. I prayed to someone I didn't believe in because I didn't know what else to do, and that prayer was answered. At a time when everything seemed dark, I looked for light—a smile, a kind gesture—anywhere I could find it, and I believed it reflected God's love. I asked for help, and I got it.

And after forty-plus years of skepticism, cynicism, and doubt, I know this too: God exists. I know it because, oddly, I see signs everywhere, including in the very places that previously seemed to be proof of the Lord's absence, or worse, the Creator's neglect of a battered, hungry, suffering creation. I don't see God making everything right. It doesn't happen in my life or anyone else's. But I do see rays of goodness that light up lonely corners, like my father's love for my increasingly confused and fragile mother and Alison Des Forges's faithful witness during the Rwanda genocide. I have seen God's purpose in Laurie and Eric's rescue of adults and children with mental disabilities and in the sacrificial love of IJM social workers for our clients, the bravery of our investigators, the skill of our lawyers in court, and the joy they all experience in this good fight.

I've learned something about churches too, and it is this:

Separatist church doctrine and exclusivity were part of my un-faith narrative for years, but I'm over it. If a church has any purpose at all, it has to be for us to help one another act like Jesus. "What Would Jesus Do?" is neither a slogan nor a cliché. It is the most profound question we will ever ask. What Jesus did was lead us to love him, to love God, and to love one another. That's what Christians should be known for. Otherwise we should shut the hell up.

I've learned that Amazing Grace—Jesus's love—can happen early in life. It can also happen after decades of loss and waste and foolishness, as it did for me, and it can happen in the last minutes of life. There are millions of words in the Bible, and many of them are confusing. But the exchange between Jesus and the thief, dying side by side, nailed to crosses, is crystal clear: The thief knew no creed or hymn or prayer; he'd memorized no verses and done few—if any—good deeds. But he knew God's face when he saw it, and he was treasured, forgiven, remembered, and saved. "Jesus, remember me when you come into your kingdom." Jesus answered him, "Truly I tell you, today you will be with me in Paradise."

The most important thing I've found on this journey is that there is a source for the courage, the joy, the patience, and the saving kindness. And when we ask that source of infinite goodness, truth, and generosity to make us more loving, braver, kinder, and more generous, those prayers are answered every time.

eleven

The Thin Year

There is a delicious Celtic phrase meaning spots where heaven and earth are very close: "thin places." I think there are "thin years," when heaven and earth are very close, where our need for God is its greatest and his presence the most palpable.

The past year was one of those for me. There were a lot of things going on in my life, but one of the most important was my friendship with Sandy, a finance officer at IJM. She's one of the few people in our young organization in my age group, and we've become fast friends. We both love to sew and quilt, and crafts were an immediate point of connection. But everybody's drawn to Sandy, quilter or not. She is so radiantly faithful, so funny, and so kind that everybody at IJM knows and loves her. Sandy lost her beloved husband, Bill, on February 15, 2012. Being her friend throughout the year since he died is what has made it a thin year for me.

Sandy and Bill loved each other for most of their adult lives, but nonetheless they went separate ways and didn't reunite and marry until Sandy was in her forties and Bill in his midfifties. They loved their Rockville, Maryland, home, their church, and their cat. Bill, who was retired, cooked gourmet meals for Sandy. So far, so normal. But then there was their insane shared passion for an unlikely assortment of things: NASCAR, the ballet, dirty martinis, the Green Bay Packers, classic black-and-white movies from the 1930s and '40s, and theology. They adored dolphins and pelicans and prayer and jokes. Bill possessed a bone-dry wit; his favorite thing was to convulse his earnest wife with verbal zingers. Anyone with eyeballs could see how amazed and grateful they were to be together. It was a glorious eighteen-year marriage.

Bill's death was brutally sudden. He had been troubled with a bad cough for months, and pulmonary specialists couldn't identify the problem. On Valentine's Day, Bill woke Sandy and said, "We're going to the hospital." Those were the last words she heard him say. By the time the ambulance arrived, Bill was in agony. Twenty-four hours later he died, holding Sandy's hand. It was lung cancer that had metastasized to his liver and other organs. No one knew until the last day of his life.

I always thought that the rules should be off for people who suffer a loss like Sandy's. Our standard of choice for good behavior in the face of life-altering grief is "holding up well." But how, actually, does one get through the first day, then the next, and then the next month, and then the outrageous prospect of the next ten then twenty years without him? Is there actually a way to hold up well with a pulverized heart and a shattered life?

Yes. When we left the hospital together after Bill died, Sandy and I talked in the parking lot in the rain before she drove to her empty house for her first hour of life as a widow. She spoke very calmly about the people she needed to call and the arrangements to make. Then she stopped and, through her tears, said, "I want all of this to honor God." What a dazzlingly faithful thing to say. Your beloved husband is gone with no warning, and you want God to be honored.

Sandy took some time off to be with Bill's beloved daughter, Ann, and her family; then she came back to work at IJM. People reached out to help with both hands, and Sandy took those hands. Her boss, Lauren, arranged a month's rotation of lunches and dinners for staff with Sandy; it was fully subscribed within a few hours. Kleenex boxes, phone calls. Martinis. Movies, cards, prayers. Many prayers: quiet ones, sobbed ones. A year of tears, a year of loneliness, a year of love.

Sandy, who leads a small group of women of whom I am one, shared her sorrow and her faith when we joined together every Wednesday morning during the thin year. One time she bowed her head, her thick gray hair swinging over her cheeks, covered her face with her hands, and said, "I know two things. I'm really sad. And God is always good." She holds these views with absolute conviction.

My uncertainty about God's goodness has always been premised on the fear that our faith is premised on the happiness of our lives. Even as someone who now believes that God is real and is good, I withhold trust, just a bit, out of perverse loyalty to those who suffer. Sandy's great trust in God in the months following Bill's death, and her dignity and generosity while she suffered the greatest loss of her life, was a revelation to me. It undermined the doubts about God's goodness in times of suffering that still cling to my soul like barnacles.

My dog Fala died a week after Bill did. I was grief stricken but embarrassed as hell to weep in the arms of a woman who had just lost her husband. Sandy, who loves animals and loves me, said, "Don't be embarrassed. Grief is grief." One Sunday afternoon we were on the phone together, and we just bawled for about an hour. Then we sniffed and blew our noses and laughed about Bill.

Heaven's comfort and earth's suffering were layered like a terrine that year. There were many horrible days, like the one when Sandy cleared out Bill's clothes and felt like she would simply never again be happy, even for a moment. And there were God-sent miracles: a school of dolphins surfaced to say good-bye just at the moment that Sandy and Ann floated an urn with Bill's ashes into the Atlantic Ocean. And sandwiched between were lonely days and good ones, depression and joy, and above all, faith. Sandy never for an instant doubted God. No, rather, in every act of kindness and affection, she felt God's goodness.

I talked with an atheist friend about finding God in all this. She said, "But don't you see? It's all people. You say it's God's love, and I say it's people's. But how would someone know God's love if it weren't for kind people? Why do you need a deity? Human love is miracle enough."

I'm remembering now when I first believed that very thing. It was the beginning of my un-faith journey, and I told you the story at the beginning of this book. My grandfather died, and my grandmother lost her faith and nearly lost her life because of her grief. It was horrifyingly clear to me that her faith was in a person, and having lost him, she lost her faith in

God. I thought about it carefully, with all the gravitas of my sixteen years, and then I consciously rejected God. It was all just people after all.

But I'm done with that view. Forty-plus years of it was enough. It isn't true for me anymore. At the end of every day, Sandy goes home to a house where Bill isn't anymore. The loving friends around her have gone for the night. But God is still there. She knows the Holy Spirit is with her, and she feels this presence especially when she is most alone.

Sandy has been my friend and teacher during this thinnest of years. One year to the day after Bill died, my own husband received a diagnosis of lung cancer. It was February 2013. John was hospitalized for the flu; a chest x-ray and CT scan revealed a small mass in his lungs. It was the news I'd been dreading for the thirty years we've been together.

I behaved very badly for a bit when I learned John had lung cancer. My first emotion was towering rage. I had long known that smoking was going to kill him. He wouldn't quit. And now my kids were going to lose their father. I think rage was a cover for fear, but there's no sugarcoating it. I was so furious with him when I learned of the diagnosis that I wanted to kill him myself. John has never been unkind or impatient with me. All he said was "I'm so sorry."

I was ashamed. He was facing surgery, possible chemotherapy and radiation, and the very real possibility of death in the near future. He quit smoking immediately. Cold turkey.

Lovely, gentle man that he is, he never mentioned it. He wasn't snarly or agitated or anxious. He just quit, quietly. It must have been hell, but I wouldn't have known.

I was only mad for a few hours after the diagnosis, but I was terrified for weeks. I had lost a good friend to lung cancer the previous summer, my guitar teacher, Scott. He was about John's age, though, unlike John, he had quit smoking decades ago. Scott was diagnosed in January and died in July, but not before the cancer metastasized to his brain. He suffered so greatly, and so did his lovely companion, Emma. I kept thinking about Grace and Josie having to witness that in their father.

At one horrible point, about a week after John was diagnosed, I slipped my spiritual moorings altogether. Erica, a young woman on my team here at IJM, stopped by my office to chat, as she does every day. We are very close; she was one of the few people I told about John's illness. I said to Erica, "I don't know what to say. I don't know how to act. What if I lose my faith like my grandmother? What if my happiness and contentment and peace were John all along?" And it seemed entirely possible, in that moment, that it would happen that way.

Erica just listened. Tears filled her eyes, and she just listened. And saying what I feared most out loud actually made my fear dissolve. I was okay after that. I asked the Holy Spirit to be with us and give us courage, calm, and kindness. That's what we got. We also got great results from pathology, which revealed that the small tumor hadn't spread at all. The surgery to remove half his lung took all the cancer with it, and he won't even have to have radiation or chemotherapy.

John got a second chance. We are grateful.

I had my own surgery this year: cataract removal from both eyes. Yes, I actually did. I've been wearing glasses since I was about six years old and am completely helpless without my bifocal Coke-bottle glasses. Cataract surgery gave me perfect vision, including a huge increase in the amount of light the new implanted lenses admit. Everything is lighter, brighter, pinker, greener.

My heart feels pinker and greener too. I feel like I had spiritual cataract surgery. Cliché, sorry, but nonetheless the only way I know how to describe it. Now that I believe in a kind and present God, that belief has changed the way I see things in the world. I see signs of God's goodness in places I never even noticed before. There is a woman named Ms. Nita who is a checker at the Safeway on Capitol Hill. Ms. Nita is about sixty-five years old. She is extraordinarily extroverted, and you can hear her loving on the people coming through her line from across the store. She is beautifully made up with extravagantly long fingernails. I have been going to that Safeway for thirty-five years. Ms. Nita has been there the whole time. I used to be embarrassed by her. Introvert and snot that I am, I would avoid her lane just in case she got chatty.

One day during a cold winter month in the thin year, I was in Ms. Nita's checkout lane. She chatted to me happily, asking after my daughters and commenting on the weather. A young man named Christopher lumbered over to help bag my groceries. Chris has a mental disability that manifests in near-constant conversation with himself, including loud laughter, jokes, and long quotations from movies. He's another Safeway employee I've avoided in the past. Ms. Nita immediately turned the full blaze of her love and care on Chris. She asked him, "What do we do when we go outside? We wear our coat! I don't want you gettin' the flu again." Then she stood on her tiptoes to tenderly button his coat under his chin.

Ms. Nita watches out for Chris. When his ramblings become too loud or he gets agitated or confused, he goes to her and she tells him what to do. "We're going to be quiet now, honey. Look at me. I love you, Chris. I'll tell you what to do. You just come right here. It's all right, darlin'. Don't I always look after you?" She lights up Christopher and the whole store with a constant stream of questions, praise, and love.

This spring, my daughter Josie and I were at Safeway, and I told Ms. Nita about my husband's surgery for lung cancer. She put down the box of crackers in her hand, said a few words to herself, then came around her register to where we stood in line. She took my hand and Josie's in each of hers, wrapping her fingers with their beautiful superlong fuchsia nails softly around ours. And she prayed out loud for John. She said,

"Lord, I lift all this up to you. Yes, Jesus. You know this family. I give this to you. I commend it to you, Lord. Mmmm, hmmm. Yes, Lord. You can do this, Lord." This went on for several minutes, right there in the middle of the grocery checkout lane.

I do not know how to measure spiritual transformation, but my feelings about Ms. Nita and hers for me are a pretty good indicator for the time being. Before I came to see God's love in the love of others, an extroverted, pray-out-loud Safeway checker was an embarrassment. And now I just want to experience in my life one small portion of the love and joy that Ms. Nita has and showers on her friends in the Safeway checkout line. God's presence among us is certain. It has changed me. Now I seek out Ms. Nita and Chris's aisle just to enjoy their banter and friendship and to be on the receiving end of one of her one-thousand-kilowatt smiles. I learn something new from Chris's inexhaustible, strange store of information every time we talk. As Ms. Nita says, "Don't you underestimate Chris. He is absolutely brilliant."

Part of seeing things differently, in faith, is gaining a different perspective on the past as well as on the present and future. This past year I have thought so much about my grandmother's mental breakdown, back when I was sixteen years old. Her suffering caused by her loss of connection with the God she worshiped was the beginning of my many years of unbelief. I believe in Tillich's definition of Providence: that there is something of God's love and care in even the most hopeless of circumstances. Having come to faith gives me the eyes to look for it.

And as I look backward to those years for a sign of his presence in the depths of my grandmother's mental illness, I see...me. I was there. I visited my grandmother often, including when she was in the worst stages of catatonic depression. I was with her before and after electroconvulsive therapy and watched her slowly come back to life. The God I did not believe in guided my feet to her bedside. Could it be possible that he sent his love to her through me—a furious, brokenhearted atheist?

My friend Amy says, "God writes straight with crooked lines." The Lord uses us, in spite or because of our foolishness, brokenness, and suffering, to do true and lovely things. I believe in that God. I can glimpse—just barely—the possibility that my grandmother's love was God's great gift to me. And my participation in her suffering was my gift to her. That's where God was in both of our lives all along.

Acknowledgments

I am grateful for friends who helped me with this book. Christine Britton, Ken Germer, Teresa Hillis, Andy Crouch, Mark Labberton, Eileen Campbell, and Erica Boonstra were my earliest readers and encouragers. Lori Foley Poer provided friendly editorial advice. My father, Laurence Burkhalter, and siblings, Kathy, Karol, Gary, and Roo, warmly supported me in this endeavor. Alex Harris believed this could be a book and convinced me. My editor Nicci Jordan Hubert pummeled me and the manuscript into order, thank goodness. Most of all, I am thankful to my husband, John. For everything.

Notes

Chapter 1

13 *plead for the widow,* Isaiah 1:17.

13 *you yourselves were being tortured,* Hebrews 13:3.

13 *the poor and needy,* Proverbs 31:8–9.

16 *love your neighbor,* "You shall love your neighbor as yourself" (Matthew 22:39).

Chapter 3

36 *not really be a community at all,* Timothy Keller, *The Reason for God: Belief in an Age of Skepticism* (New York: Penguin, 2008), 40.

37 *The answer is nothing,* Robin R. Meyers, *Saving Jesus from the Church: How to Stop Worshiping Christ and Start Following Jesus* (New York: HarperOne, 2009), 134–35.

39 *for our learning,* C. S. Lewis, *Reflections on the Psalms* (New York: Harcourt, 1964), 22.

39 *pursue me,* Job 19:21–22.

43 *wipe out every breathing creature,* 1 Samuel 15:3.

44 *you yourselves were being tortured,* Hebrews 13:3.

45 *epic human rights report,* Alison Liebhafsky Des Forges,
    Leave None to Tell the Story: Genocide in Rwanda,
    Human Rights Watch, March 1, 1999, www.hrw.org
    /reports/1999/03/01/leave-none-tell-story.

50 *killer executioners,* Scott Macleod, "The Life and Death
    of Kevin Carter," *Time,* September 12, 1994, www
    .time.com/time/magazine/article/0,9171,981431,00
    .html.

Chapter 4

59 *Fates is determined,* Charles Dickens, *Martin Chuzzle-
    wit* (New York: Penguin Classics, 2000).

59 *change agents,* Ann Voskamp, *One Thousand Gifts: A
    Dare to Live Fully Right Where You Are* (Grand Rapids:
    Zondervan, 2011), 58.

61 *the one who lifts a finger,* Deborah Kotz, "Why the Pope
    Is Wrong About Condoms: An Interview with South
    African Bishop Kevin Dowling, an AIDS Activist,"
    U.S. News & World Report, April 10, 2008, www.us
    news.com/news/articles/2008/04/10/why-the-pope
    -is-wrong-about-condoms.

Chapter 5

70 *the two best prayers I know,* Anne Lamott, *Traveling
    Mercies: Some Thoughts on Faith* (New York: Pantheon,
    1999), 82.

Chapter 6

77 *tries unsuccessfully to fill this void,* Blaise Pascal, *Pensées and Other Writings,* trans. Honor Levi, Oxford World's Classics (Oxford: Oxford University Press, 2008), 52.

78 *breathtaking contribution to poetry, music, and art,* Kay Redfield Jamison, *Touched with Fire: Manic-Depressive Illness and the Artistic Temperament,* rev. ed. (New York: Free Press, 1996).

79 *scattering them all over creation,* Barbara Cooney, *Miss Rumphius* (New York: Puffin Books, 1985).

Chapter 7

93 *by reason of religion,* Samantha Power, "The Enforcer: A Christian Lawyer's Global Crusade," *The New Yorker,* January 19, 2009, www.newyorker.com/reporting /2009/01/19/090119fa_fact_power.

Chapter 8

109 *He refuses to work alone,* Watchman Nee, *Let Us Pray* (Fort Washington, PA: Christian Crusade Literature, 1995), 11.

110 *I will not believe,* John 20:25.

115 *signs and wonders,* John 4:48.

116 *Wilt thou refuse,* Mother Teresa, *Come Be My Light: The Private Writings of the Saint of Calcutta,* ed. Brian Kolodiejchuk (New York: Doubleday, 2007), 98.

118   *I help souls,* Mother Teresa, *Come Be My Light,* 210.

118   *long years of interior darkness,* Mother Teresa, *Come Be My Light,* 2.

118   *Heaven from every side is closed,* Mother Teresa, *Come Be My Light,* 202.

118   *here I am Lord,* Mother Teresa, *Come Be My Light,* 188.

119   *unwanted—unloved,* Mother Teresa, *Come Be My Light,* 158, 164, 169, 186–87.

120   *a much greater disease is,* Mother Teresa, *Come Be My Light,* 296.

Chapter 9

126   *neural pathways,* Curt Thompson, *Anatomy of the Soul: Surprising Connections Between Neuroscience and Spiritual Practices That Can Transform Your Life and Relationships* (Carol Stream, IL: Tyndale, 2010), 133.

129   *every living thing,* Psalm 145:9, 14, 16, KJV.

130   *of such different kinds,* C. S. Lewis, *The Last Battle,* The Chronicles of Narnia (1956; repr. New York: Harper Trophy, 1994), 189.

135   *drove Legion into the wilds,* See Mark 5:1–20; Luke 8:26–39.

138   *I belonged to God,* Henri J. M. Nouwen, *Adam, God's Beloved* (Maryknoll, NY: Orbis Books, 1997).

141 *separate us from the love of God,* Paul Tillich, *The Shaking of the Foundations* (New York: Scribner's, 1948), 106.

Chapter 10

153 *the slave does it,* Matthew 8:5–9.

156 *there in front of me was the answer,* Caldwell B. Esselstyn Jr., *Prevent and Reverse Heart Disease: The Revolutionary, Scientifically Proven, Nutrition-Based Cure* (New York: Avery, 2007).

161 *nothing but pitiless indifference,* Richard Dawkins, *River out of Eden: A Darwinian View of Life* (New York: Basic Books, 1995).

166 *know the Law of Nature,* C. S. Lewis, *Mere Christianity* (New York: HarperOne, 2012), 10.

171 *with me in Paradise,* Luke 23:42–43.